fences
walls & gates

By Scott Atkinson and the Editors of Sunset Books,
Menlo Park, California

Sunset Books

vice president, general manager:
Richard A. Smeby

vice president, editorial director:
Bob Doyle

production director:
Lory Day

director of operations:
Rosann Sutherland

sales development director:
Linda Barker

executive editor:
Bridget Biscotti Bradley

art director:
Vasken Guiragossian

Staff for this book:

developmental editor:
Linda J. Selden

copy editor:
Phyllis Elving

photo director/stylist:
JoAnn Masaoka Van Atta

art director/page layout:
Kathy Avanzino Barone

illustrator:
Bill Oetinger

principal photographer:
E. Andrew McKinney

prepress coordinator:
Eligio Hernandez

proofreader:
Mary Roybal

Beautiful boundaries

This new Sunset book highlights the latest looks in fences, walls, and gates—all in one easy-access package. You'll see scores of color photos that paint the broad spectrum of fence styles and solutions. But you'll find more than just pretty pictures—we've included both a hard-working shopper's guide and a basic building primer, too.

Many retailers, design professionals, and homeowners shared their knowledge with us or allowed us to photograph their products and creations. We'd especially like to thank Southern Lumber Company of San

Jose, California; T&H Building Supply, Inc. of Redwood City, California; and Northern California Fence of Redwood City, California.

For the names of designers, architects, and photographers whose work is featured in this book, turn to pages 126–127.

10 9 8 7 6 5 4 3
First printing January 2004
Copyright © 2004, Sunset Publishing Corporation,
Menlo Park, CA 94025. First edition. All rights reserved, including
the right of reproduction in whole or in part in any form.

ISBN 0-376-01759-7
Library of Congress Control Number: 2003109806
Printed in the United States of America.

For additional copies of Fences, Walls & Gates or any other Sunset book,
call 1-800-526-5111 or visit us at www.sunset.com.

Cover: Crisp white pickets and posts march toward a matching garden gate and arbor. Cover design by Vasken Guiragossian. Photography by Brian Vanden Brink.

contents

getting started

THE FIRST THING to consider when you are planning to build a fence, wall, or gate is just what you want it to do. Fences can define space, edit views, and screen out wind and noise. They can keep intruders out and kids safely in. Walls serve these functions, too, and perform them with an even greater sense of permanence—some of the world's oldest structures are walls. Gates direct traffic and draw the eye to views, leading the way through fences and walls—or simply tying one inviting space to another.

Defining your basic purpose will guide you in making design and material choices. What's your preference? Cheery picket fence, rustic stone wall, bright blue entry gate? You'll find scores of styles illustrated in "Great Fences, Walls & Gates," starting on page 11. But before you begin browsing, take time to ponder the following basic points.

BORDER OR BARRIER?

Your new structure can be tall or short, open or solid. Sometimes total security is the ticket; in other situations, you may prefer just a hint of defined space. Besides the basic style and materials for your fence or wall, you'll also want to think about privacy, views (good or bad), noise, and landscaping.

In a broad sense, security fencing encompasses any fence designed to keep people in or out of a designated area. Such a fence should be tall, sturdy, and tough to climb. Psychology plays an important part in the design of a good security fence, too. A solid-board fence

This tall adobe wall could have seemed closed and cold, but open "windows," fireplace, and other Southwest touches bring it to life.

Wood fence, block wall, and curved, slatted gate. they're all tied together by crisp white wood trim and a long, straight arbor.

or brick wall may be a more effective psychological deterrent than a chain-link fence, simply because one can't see what's on the other side.

To contain children within an area such as a play yard, a fence or wall needs to be sturdy and offer no toeholds for climbing. Small wire mesh (with openings no wider than 2 inches) is ideal for play yards—its open design lets parents keep an eye on their children, but the small holes make it hard to climb over.

Fences meant to serve as privacy barriers are most effective, of course, if you can't see over, under, around, or through them. But you can avoid the feeling of a boxed-in space by giving some forethought to design and location. A series of high-and-low or open-and-closed sections can block unwanted views (and peering neighbors) while preserving desirable vistas beyond the yard. For instance,

you could use solid fence sections where you want to block the line of sight, open sections (transparent glass, wire, or spaced boards or pickets) where you want to be able to look out. Gates can serve as frames for views, too. Louver fences (see page 73) can be effective in blocking undesirable views while at the same time allowing air circulation.

Within a yard, low or open fences and walls can physically separate areas used for work, play, and relaxation from garden planting areas while still visually preserving the sense of an unbroken landscape. Use taller screening to hide unattractive sights such as trash or service areas, work centers, or swimming pool equipment.

When it comes to muting noise, one rule always applies: the thicker or higher the barrier, the more effective it will be. It should have an unbroken surface (solid masonry works best of all), and any open spaces between fence boards or panels need to be covered with lath strips. Of course, there are practical—and sometimes legal—limits to how high and thick a wall or fence can be. But even if a barrier reduces the actual noise level only slightly, it may

A formal lath fence, dressed in bright wisteria,
steps down a slope toward the street below.

seem a lot quieter when you can't see what's making the noise. The trickling murmur from a wall fountain or garden pond can help mask noise, too.

How's the weather?

A fence or wall can effectively control the elements of wind and sun to create a pleasant environment in your yard. The first thing you'll want to do is learn how the sun and wind affect your property at various times of the year; then plan your structure's design and location accordingly.

Surprisingly, a solid barrier provides little wind protection across large expanses of yard—the wind simply vaults over it and continues at the same velocity a few feet downwind. Tests have shown, though, that a fence with an open design (spaced boards or slats, louvers, or woven lath) breaks up a steady wind into a series of eddies or small breezes. Compared with a solid structure, such a fence protects a larger area from the main force of the wind.

Fences and walls can be designed to admit full sunlight, provide partial shade, or let in no sun at all. Transparent glass or plastic screens offer maximum light and a clear view while supplying wind protection around patios and decks. You can reduce heat and glare by using tinted or glare-reducing glass or plastic, which cuts the intensity of the sun's rays yet still allows a view to the other side. Latticework or other open designs provide partial or filtered shade.

Remember that the sun's path changes during the year—high in summer, low in winter. Your yard's shade patterns will vary accordingly. One solution for combating intense summer sun is to extend deciduous plantings above your permanent fence line—in winter, their bare branches will allow welcome rays to pass through. Or use removable, or even adjustable, fence panels or louvers to seasonally tailor your wind and weather.

LAYOUT LOGISTICS

If every lot were free of obstructions, as smooth as a baseball field, and measurable in even increments of 6 or 8 feet, laying out a fence would be pretty simple. But sometimes you have to figure out how to get that fence up a slope, around a tree or curve, or across a ditch or depression.

If your yard runs uphill, you can lay out a fence in one of two basic ways: follow the land's natural contours or stairstep your fence in sections. Some styles that adapt especially well to contour fencing are post-and-rail fences (see page 76) and solid fences using pickets, palings, or grapestakes. Though more difficult to design and build, geometric stepped fences (see facing page) are good solutions for board, louver, basketweave, and panel designs.

Sometimes walls are better than fences at handling obstacles—especially dry stone walls or other casual structures without footings. Stepped footings (page 83) are the solution for formal masonry units such as brick, concrete, and mortared stone.

Not all walls and fences show straight-arrow behavior. The rustic, split-rail fence design above takes sloped contours in stride—just like its modern rail-fence relatives.

Below, a colorful concrete wall zigzags down a paved poolside path. A collection of teacups adds a fun flourish.

WHERE WILL THE GATE GO?

Deciding where to locate your gate is usually pretty simple—most gates are placed for convenience. For example, you'll need a gate if your fence intersects a walk or driveway. Study your yard layout, considering possible additions or changes that might affect traffic patterns. Then decide on where a gate would best fit into the fence line. In new landscaping, gate locations will be dictated by the overall landscape plan.

A gate can either match a fence or contrast with it. Sometimes gates are made inconspicuous for security reasons, but more often it's done to avoid an unattractive break in the fence line. Conversely, a gate can be designed to call attention to itself in order to lead visitors to the entrance. Front entry gates often are designed as showpieces, reflecting the artistic tastes of their owners.

Once you've homed in on the location and basic design of your gate, you'll need to decide what size it should be. That will depend on the height of the fence or wall the gate serves and the width of the walk, path, or driveway it must span. Think about the type of traffic that must pass through it. Walk-though gates should provide clearance for yard maintenance equipment (such as wheelbarrows and garden tractors), garden furniture, and other large items that are periodically moved in and out. Consider 36 inches about the minimum. Wider gates—such as an entry where two people might pass each other—should be at least 60 inches wide. A common solution for wide openings is a double gate opening from the middle, especially if the design calls for solid, heavy gate construction.

Which way a gate should swing will be influenced both by its location and by the design of the fence or wall on which it's hung. Entry gates usually swing in toward the house or driveway; likewise, gates in boundary fences swing into your property. A gate within your property can swing in the direction of greater traffic flow. On sloped ground, hang the gate to swing toward the downhill side so it can easily clear the ground.

For safety, a gate that opens onto stairs should ideally be placed at the top rather than the bottom and should swing away from the steps.

A recycled Mexican gate is the centerpiece of this rose-draped, adobe-walled entry courtyard.

A protective fence, matching gate, and cottage-style arbor help enclose a swimming pool area.

CONSIDER THE CODES

Before you make specific plans for the size, design, and location of your structure, look into the local codes and ordinances that may influence your decisions. Requirements and restrictions will vary considerably from state to state, city to city, and even neighborhood to neighborhood. The most obvious source of information is your local building department or community planning office. Landscape professionals are also familiar with local building codes.

Regulations of some sort regarding the use of barbed wire, electric fencing, glass, and other potentially hazardous materials are almost universal. Codes are likely to dictate the design of fences near traffic intersections, and there will probably be code-imposed setback distances from buildings, property lines, or the street.

Various ordinances limit the height of fences around yards. Although restrictions vary from one community to the next, front-yard fencing is generally limited to 4 feet in height, and backyard fencing to between 6 and 8 feet. Some communities allow the standard fence height to be exceeded if the extended portion is composed of wire mesh, lattice, or other open work.

From the time the first fence was built to define a property line, such barriers have provoked many a dispute both in and out of court. To help minimize potential conflicts, it's wise to make a written agreement with your present neighbors concerning fence design and location; if possible, try to enlist their active cooperation in building the fence. One way to avoid ill feelings is to build a fence that looks as good on their side as on your own.

GREAT FENCES, WALLS & GATES

Now it's time to present some pictures. Your new structure can be constructed of wood, wire, steel, or masonry; you'll see examples of each on the following pages. You'll also find entry gates, garden gates, and gates that don't actually lead anywhere in particular. WHAT'S YOUR STYLE? Post-and-rail fences and dry stone walls have a rustic look; a mortared brick wall or white picket gate says "tradition." Concrete walls and board fences add a contemporary touch. If in doubt about what will look best, try to match the style of your house and the surrounding landscape. Remember that just a few custom touches—like a rose arbor, curved wood trim, or a dash of color—can make your fence, wall, or gate not just a barrier, but part of your home. IF YOU'RE THINKING of doing the construction yourself, you'll also want to take a look at "Building Basics," beginning on page 61. See some hardware or materials you'd like to learn more about? Turn to "A Shopper's Guide," pages 101–125.

wood & wire

DEPENDING ON whether they're tall or short, closed or open, fences can form secure barriers or inviting borders. Build them from wood, metal, or a combination of the two. Compared to walls, fences generally go up faster and cost less.

Board fences may be old standbys, but these days you'll find them dancing new steps. Paint them, stain them, let them weather naturally, or festoon them with flowers. Picket patterns offer myriad variations on the classic white theme. Rail fences evoke the rural past. Lath and lattice offer open views, improved air flow, and a leg up for climbing plants. Go even more rustic with bentwood twigs, woven willow or wattle, and a plethora of bamboo styles.

And what about the wire that won the West? Barbed wire is no longer allowed in most places, but welded wire, poultry netting, and wire mesh products are direct descendants. Use them with metal stakes or, for a more finished look, framed with wood. Try weaving wood strips or plants through utilitarian chain-link fencing. Steel, vinyl, and aluminum fences are also available, as is that most traditional of metal fences—wrought iron.

If you're of an eclectic bent, there's no reason to stop there: fence materials are where you find them. What about copper plumbing pipe, corrugated metal siding, recycled tree stakes, or other flea-market finds?

A classic white post-and-rail fence strides past showy spring blossoms, covering a lot of ground while using a minimum of materials.

This cozy, whorled-brick pocket patio is backed by a vertical-board fence topped with lattice. The latticework provides added privacy without the closed-in feel of a tall, solid fence.

An entry boardwalk winds past screenlike fences (above) staggered to form a "friendly barrier." The colorful horizontal panels are made from Bakelite covered with a thin, painted wood veneer. At right, vertical louvers form an open patio screen that allows light, air, and a bit of a view to pass through.

Board fences may be common, but they don't all need to look the same. The good-neighbor fence above alternates boards, making it equally good-looking on both sides. Fast-growing trees, 5 feet apart, offer extra privacy only two years after being planted. At right, fluted joints and a "piano-key" top section add a touch of openness to a green-painted Craftsman fence. Below, rustic grapestakes fill in between more formal brick pilasters.

These two fences use different tricks to deal with grades.
The enclosure shown above, combining horizontal
panels with vertical slats, perches atop a stone
retaining wall, screening a courtyard patio from the
street. The crisscross lath fence at right steps down,
section by section, to a flanking stone pillar.

A formal lath screen mirrors the arch of a hardwood patio bench, adding both style and privacy without too much sense of enclosure.

These two fence designs depart from tradition. The dye-stained poles at left—in mixed colors and sizes—are strung together with plumber's tape. Above, flexible redwood benderboard, woven into a horizontal basketweave pattern, takes a tight curve.

Picket fences come in all sorts of shapes and colors. The classic contour at left combines wide boards with a gentle reverse arc on top. At bottom left, it's the rails that curve, not the beveled 2 by 2 uprights. Below, intricate infill includes custom crisscrosses. The plain-Jane pattern at bottom right makes up for its simplicity with brash red makeup.

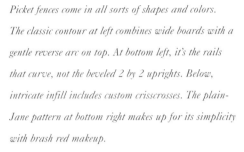

*Here are three more picket patterns—all featuring
classy, mirror-image edge cutouts. The intricate sawn
pickets at left border on the Gothic, while those below left
make a more restrained statement. Below right,
furniture-like infill matches massive, weathered posts
and kickboard.*

Bamboo can take on many forms as a fence. The diamond-pattern fence shown above includes a gracefully curved top rail; the screen at right forms a solid backdrop for a Japanese maple.

Wattle fences are cottage-garden classics. This one is sculpted from thin, supple willow branches woven around thicker uprights.

Branches, twigs, and poles make fun, rustic fences
The so-called "coyote fence" above sits atop a stucco
knee wall, complementing a bright blue gate. The garden
enclosure at right combines rough rails and pole posts
with delicate bentwood infill.

Traditional steel and wrought-iron fences evoke bygone times. Though some metal fences are available "off-the-shelf," most are custom-built by skilled craftspersons. The patterns above and at left are just two options.

Sure, chain-link fencing can be boring, but it can also form a secure backdrop for more elegant camouflage—like the flowering shrubs and border plants woven through this fence.

*The welded-wire fence
at left combines an
open feel with just
enough style to look
good—thanks to the
thick, wide-spaced
posts with copper post
caps. Below, a formal
wood-and-metal
design pairs a sturdy,
slatted frame with
painted steel top
sections.*

The bedstead below grew new wings when recycled as a planting-bed border. At right, aluminum slats were woven horizontally around existing steel fence bars.

The open-style fence and gate at right feature a weathered frame of redwood posts and rails, plus infill of steel electrical conduit. (You could also try copper plumbing pipe.)

First painted, then encouraged to stain, corrugated metal siding (left) took on a rustic patina. Above, old wheels hang from fencing wire—there's no telling where collectibles stop and the fence begins.

masonry walls

WALLS ARE MORE FORMAL, more permanent, and in some ways more architectural than fences. Walls also follow slopes well—especially those built from small masonry units, like bricks. Masonry goes well with wood, too; why not combine a wall and a fence in the same yard, or even in the same structure?

Brick and stone are the classics. Depending on the type of brick you choose and the way it's laid out, a brick wall can be highly formal or a bit casual. Stone is still more rustic—especially a dry-stacked flagstone or fieldstone wall. On the other hand, trimmed, mortared ashlar stone offers a formal alternative to brick.

Poured concrete is the modern miracle material. Concrete walls generally look more austere than brick or stone, but they can be textured, colored, or otherwise personalized to ease their sometimes monolithic look.

Concrete garden walls, dressed in sunny Caribbean colors, join with "windows" of glass block and wire to border a courtyard dining area.

Recycled glass adds a blast of color to this concrete retaining wall.

Two other masonry units—one old, one new—round out the basic collection. Adobe conveys the unmistakable tang of the Southwest. Concrete blocks go up quickly and can be veneered with colorful stucco, stone, brick, or tile.

Glass block is another way to break up a blank stretch of wall. Use it for complete wall sections or for "windows" within a wall. Plants also help soften a stark masonry wall (see pages 44–51). Or add some finishing touches (pages 52–59), such as a wall fountain, a built-in bench, or trompe l'oeil artwork.

Flow-through openings add light and air to otherwise blank masonry walls. Staggered chinks in formal, mortared brick (left) show Old World flair. Terra-cotta drain tiles (above) form masonry "windows" atop solid brick sections.

A Southwest sitting area's mortared adobe walls set the stylistic theme; the painted window section and built-in adobe seating shelf make it special.

A classic, used-brick wall (right) highlights impeccable masonry work. Built-in planting beds overflow with spring bulbs and other flowers.

Dry-stacked stone walls are less formal alternatives to mortared brick. A winding fieldstone wall (facing page) evokes a classic rural feel. Seven foot-tall walls of buff-colored Utah sandstone (above) keep a courtyard garden safe from deer and other wayward munchers.

Mortared stone walls look great, too. Above, a formal, fitted, stone-capped wall negotiates courtyard curves. At left, river rocks are seeded in mortar like raisins in pudding.

These painted concrete monoliths are open and playful,
forming screens, windows, and planter beds while directing
the eye upward and outward.

Don't throw out that
old, broken concrete—
instead, recycle it into
a rustic, stonelike
garden wall like the
one shown here.

A rough-surfaced, form-stamped concrete entry wall is highlighted by a shielded fluorescent fixture.

A faux-painted finish brings fresh interior design style to a shady garden corner. The stucco wall covering, with subtle integral color, was applied over an old, tired-out wooden fence.

A quiet, sun-dappled sitting area (above) combines lush plantings with a blue stucco backdrop. A brasher blue pool barrier (left) features a handcrafted tile mosaic.

Walls can be primly rectangular or loosely curved. At right, a lemon yellow, stuccoed-block retaining wall steps down to street level but has open, painted-lattice fencing up at front-yard level. The snow-mantled adobe wall below flows up and over a gaily-painted yellow gate.

great fences, walls & gates

great gates

GATES, OF COURSE, lead the way through walls and fences. They also welcome guests, frame views, and provide garden accents—either formal or fun. Gates can have real personalities, too, as you'll see on the following pages.

Entry gates welcome visitors to your door and can make unique design statements. Consider using a material that stands out: how about custom wrought iron, frame-and-panel hardwood, or decorative etched glass? Pay attention to the gate latch or knob—it's the first thing guests reach for. Arbors and trellises are frequent companions to entry gates. (For planting ideas, see pages 44–51.)

Smaller garden gates can blend in subtly or stand out in quirky glory. Maybe you'd like a redwood gate that matches your board fence, with just an arched top to set it off; perhaps a traditional white picket gate with classic black hardware is more your style. Or go casual: try bamboo with hemp hinges; an antique metal screen with pointed wood posts; or a recycled, multipaned door or brightly painted window.

You don't even need a wall or fence in order to have a gate. Try setting flanking gate posts, adding some stepping stones through the opening, and planting right up to the posts to shape a gated "pathway" through yard or garden. Design a see-through gate to frame a view, or make it more opaque to offer just a hint as to what's behind it.

Install spiked gate posts, lay down some stepping stones, and add a recycled metal gate from the flea market—there's no clear destination here, except for wherever the cat has in mind.

This white picket gate with arched hedge looks quite formal, but why not cut a playful rabbit in one of the scrolled picket tops?

*It's a classic cottage-garden picture—
complete with white picket gate, black-
iron gate hardware, and an over-arching
arbor dense with roses.*

*Here are two more distinctive
interpretations of the entry-gate theme.
On the facing page, a handhewn, solid-
wood gate is tucked below a plastered-
adobe arch with flanking carriage
lamps. At right, a Craftsman-style
home has a bold gate, arbor, and fence
built to match.*

Part gate, part space frame: the sculptural steel structure above is flanked by striking granite boulders. In quiet contrast, the carved frame-and-panel gate at right swings within matching gate posts.

At right, an Arizona take on the classic "moon gate" includes ornamental steel agave, ironwood, and saguaro figures inside an arch of native stone.

Above, double driveway gates sport curved hardwood rails and flanking stone pilasters. In the gate at right, "oak branches" of patinaed copper were fashioned to match the forest beyond. The surrounding fence and arbor, with their open design of weathered wood, offer unobstructed views.

The rustic twig gate above opens to a lush cottage garden. At right, a freestanding, furniture-grade gate sits stoically in the winter snow.

A recycled door (top) is part gate, part casual garden accent. In contrast, a formal front gate (above) incorporates traditional details— like the wrought-iron counterweight that keeps it closed.

The garden structure at left is all "found objects," including a pair of salvaged bifold doors and two old windows used to form the peaked arch. Below, copper rabbits hop from one side of matched copper doors to the other.

Simple gates can be striking. The painted pickets at left are a classic counterpart to both aged stone walls and ephemeral flowers. Above, a bamboo gate with traditional twine hinges is angled to play off the fence line.

living
fences

D RESS YOUR FENCE or wall with colorful plants—or, if you prefer, shape a fence entirely from plants. Either way, the distinction between garden and barrier melts away.

Arbors and trellises are great partners for fences, walls, and gates. Extending plants above the fence line is a tried-and-true way to gain privacy beyond the maximum allowable fence height. Let tall fence posts do double duty as arbor posts, or add new posts in front or back. "Float" a lath trellis a few inches from the fence to support plants; or simply string wire. Build a classic, arching arbor above your gate to give climbing roses a purchase. Weave plantings in and out of a chain-link fence to muffle noise as well as camouflage the fencing material.

Or use plants alone as your fence. A classic boxwood hedge, apple arbor, or crisscross live-willow fence brings the landscape within reach. Give plants a helping hand by stretching poultry netting or single strands of green-coated wire between stakes or posts.

Even simpler: combine planter boxes or planting niches with an existing structure. Add a built-in planter box at the base or even the top of a fence. Pack the niches between wall stones with soil, then plant succulents there. Hang colorful containers or planter baskets on a board fence. Or train shrubs in formal shapes, espalier style, along a painted stucco wall.

'Polka' rose canes, trained along three wires, form this fence. They're simply strung between sturdy posts with decorative metal caps.

The board fence that forms the midsection of this enclosure serves mostly as a support for lush plant growth above and below. The trellis on top has horizontal wire supports for vines, which spill all the way down to the stacked-log planters along the fence base.

Stone pillars, white picket fence, and gate
come together in a Southern scene with a showy,
sturdy rose arch as its centerpiece.

Dry-stacked stone walls can harbor all sorts
of plants—above, soil for succulents was packed
into wall crevices. At right, 'Lady Banks' climbing
roses cover an 8-foot-tall, 16-foot-diameter steel
frame, creating an enclosed outdoor room
for reading and relaxation.

Bright red roses are often trained on arbors, but here the plants are the only thing that's visible: two 'Blaze' roses completely covered the underlying iron arch within two years.

Golden bamboo quickly forms a thick living fence; a mirror at the end of this tunnel extends the small garden into infinity.

Above, ocotillo uprights form a flowering fence, supported by 6-foot steel posts and steel bars. Ocotillo "panels" were wired together on top, with the bottom ends buried 6 inches in the ground— where they took root.

At far left, live willows
were woven in crisscross
fashion. A looming
evergreen hedge (near left)
shields a side yard from
the neighbors' view.

Petunias (above) were packed in flexible plastic planter pouches filled with moistened, compressed potting medium, then hung directly on the fence. For a casual cottage-garden border, use poultry netting or hardware cloth as a transparent fence (right).

The fence at left gains lots of vertical real estate via flying arbors and flanking, bracing trellises. Above, simple box planters line a brightly-painted picket fence. The 7-foot-tall stucco wall below is trimmed with espaliered apple trees rooted in built-in planter boxes.

great fences, walls & gates

details, details

P<small>LANTS CAN</small> customize a fence or wall (see pages 44–51), but there are other ways to give it a personal stamp, too. The following flourishes might help you "soften" your structure or use it as a focal point.

Windows or other openings edit views, add depth, and break up a tall, blank barrier with touches of light and air. A built-in bench offers a spot to linger or serves as a platform for container plants—anchor a wood bench to your fence frame, cantilever a stone slab, or build a masonry shelf out from the wall's base. An extra-deep garden gate might be flanked on each side by short benches.

At night, light up your structure with uplights embedded in the patio or planting bed; downlights aimed from an arbor or fencetop; shielded lights washing a wall for texture; or decorative rope lights sparkling along a gate arch. Candles and candle lanterns can add garden ambience after hours. A trickling wall fountain or waterfall helps mask neighborhood noises; all you need to create one is a small garden-pond pump.

And why not use your wall or fence as an artist's canvas "painted" with planters, tile murals, birdhouses—or even real paintings? Embed treasured old cups and saucers, wine bottles, or other collectibles in concrete or mortar. Mirrors add sparkle, and large ones seem to stretch garden space.

Post caps can add a finishing flourish to fence tops or deck rails. Make your own or choose from a growing list of ready-made models. The caps below are high-fired ceramic.

This artful garden wall was fashioned from gleaming stainless steel that shimmers with reflected light and subtle color. The art "gallery" features photos of plants printed on sheets of steel using a special emulsion process.

Recessed, sealed well lights graze freestanding concrete walls from below, forming a soft, textured backdrop for alfresco dining. Candles add their warm, decorative glow atop the table.

Here's an easy and subtle way to add night light to a fence: hollow wood sleeves with low-voltage bulbs built in. Each unit slips over the top of any tall 4-by-4 post, leaving enough room for the power cord.

A multipaned window (below) set over a built-in stone bench is backlit to glow from behind. Against a rustic backyard stucco wall (facing page), water spills out of scalloped bowls amidst blazing bougainvillea. Even a tranquil trickle will help mask neighborhood noise.

A wall-side arbor supports both
roses and an inviting patio swing
(above) while also blocking the
view of the neighbor's house behind
the wall. At right, a stucco wall in
terra-cotta color features a subtle
built-in bench.

Openings add interest to a concrete wall (left), a louvered fence top (above), and a steel "moon gate" (right). Use them to frame a view, edit a view, or let in light.

This stone sitting slab leans out from a matching wall, forming a sturdy perch for both people and plantings.

A lath fence (left)
supports climbing ivy
and provides openings
just the right size for
terra-cotta flower pots.
The tile mural below
brings a vista from
a favored vacation
spot to a sheltered
courtyard wall.

A niche or holder for a
candle (top) can bring
a cozy feel to a wall or
fence come nighttime.
An amber-colored wine
bottle (above) glows
from a mortared wall.

Bored with your fence? Use it as a backdrop for artwork or other collectibles. The lattice fence above serves as a canvas to display a collection of colorful birdhouses. At right, carved wooden fish swim across shingled fence siding.

Some views are great, but if yours isn't, think of adding one you like better. This adobe wall's "window" suggests a grand mountain vista beyond— a spot where painted bears perpetually roam.

BUILDING BASICS

Can you build that fence, wall, or gate yourself? That's where this chapter comes in. You'll find the basic steps for building all three types of structures on the following pages; tailor these procedures to your specific situation. Fence building and masonry are straightforward tasks that require only basic tools and techniques. They do, however, take both planning and energy. For this reason, it's wise to have some help; if necessary, ask a neighbor or hire a laborer to work beside you. Gate-building can be a bit more leisurely: you can build a gate at your own pace in the garage, then take it out to install it in place when you're ready. Whatever you're constructing, the first step will be to acquire a building permit, if one is required. Then make your materials list and begin shopping; "A Shopper's Guide," beginning on page 101, will help you select what you need. Finally, gather up both your plans and your tools, head outside, and start building.

BUILDING A FENCE

MOST FENCING JOBS fall into three stages: the relatively easy preliminary stage of plotting the fence, the somewhat more difficult process of installing posts, and the straight-forward final step of adding the rails and siding. BASIC BUILDING methods for all three fencing stages are outlined in this section; you can adjust these procedures to fit your needs. WE'LL ALSO SHOW you some specific construction details for various types of fences, beginning on page 74.

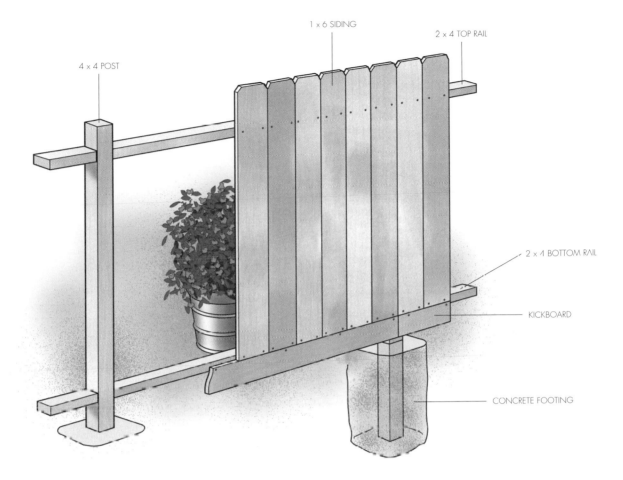

4 x 4 POST

1 x 6 SIDING

2 x 4 TOP RAIL

2 x 4 BOTTOM RAIL

KICKBOARD

CONCRETE FOOTING

Fence anatomy

The key to a successful fence is a strong, square frame.
The classic board fence, shown above, is 6 feet high, with
a frame of 4-by-4 posts set 6 feet apart on center and 2 by
4 rails nailed between the posts. The posts are 8 feet long,
set in concrete about 2 feet in the ground. To help support
the weight of the boards, the bottom rail is sometimes
placed on edge (see page 71). Extra-heavy fences may
require a third rail.

Vertical board siding is the standby, nailed or screwed to
both the top and bottom rails. Of course, siding makes the
fence, and you'll discover many different treatments
throughout this book.

Sometimes a kickboard is installed below the bottom
rail to close the gap between the fence and the ground.
The kickboard, like the siding, is usually made from 1-by
lumber.

Taking stock

Before you set a post or drive a nail, check local building
and zoning codes (see page 9), which may influence fence
style, materials, setback, and other considerations. For a
fence that's on or near a boundary line, it's wise to have a
surveyor or civil engineer lay out the corner stakes unless
you're absolutely certain where the property line is.

To be sure you're not going to hit any pipelines or
underground cables when you dig, have your utility compa-
nies mark the locations of cables and pipes.

Going shopping

For a long-lived, weatherproof fence, choose either
pressure-treated wood (which has had preservatives forced
deeply into it) or redwood, cedar, or some kinds of cypress
Specify heartwood (page 102)—it's decay- and insect-resis-
tant. Use only rust-proof hardware—hot-dipped galvanized

building basics

TOOLS OF THE TRADE: FENCES

Whatever fencing design you choose, the basic tools are the same. You'll need a long tape measure (16 to 25 feet is best), a 50- to 100-foot reel tape, and a water level or line level for plotting the fence line; a spool of mason's twine or string; and a plumb bob to mark post locations accurately. You'll need a posthole digger, auger, or power auger for digging, and a carpenter's level (2 feet or longer) for aligning posts.

You'll also need a carpenter's square, a hammer, a power circular saw or crosscut saw, a butt chisel, a portable drill and the appropriate drill bits for boring pilot holes and mortising posts, and a shovel to fill postholes with concrete or earth and gravel. Add a small garden spade for

removing excess earth from postholes, a jigsaw (saber saw) for cutting pickets, and a wheelbarrow for mixing concrete. A power reciprocating saw comes in handy when cutting posts in place.

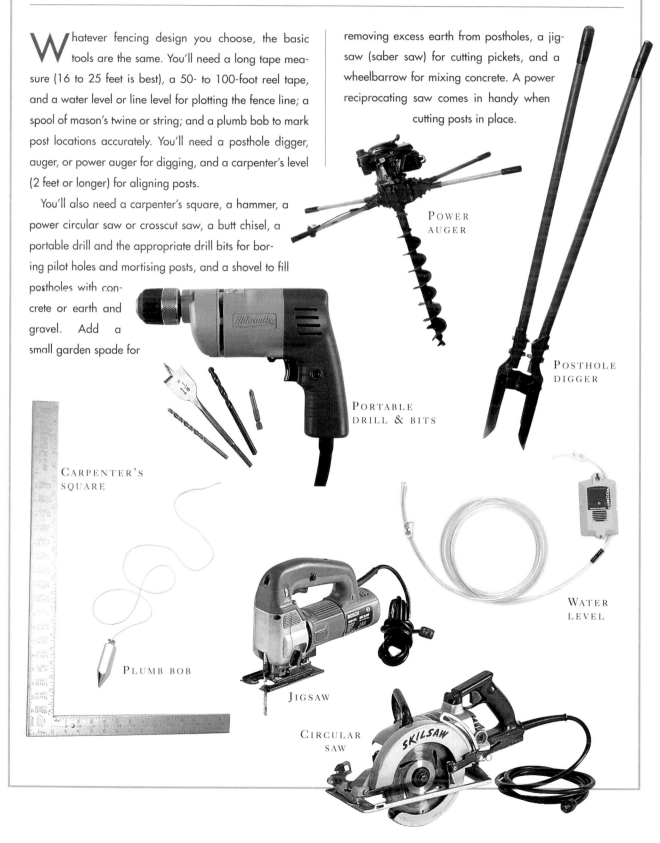

POWER
AUGER

POSTHOLE
DIGGER

PORTABLE
DRILL & BITS

WATER
LEVEL

CARPENTER'S
SQUARE

PLUMB BOB

JIGSAW

CIRCULAR
SAW

nails or deck screws, galvanized bolts, fence brackets, and other connectors.

Before you shop, take the time to sketch your proposed fence design, calling out all lumber types and sizes, heights and widths, fasteners, and finishes. To make planning and shopping easier, focus on a single fence section—say, a 6-foot-long bay—and count up all the materials in that section. Then simply count the fence sections and multiply your materials list by that number. Add in some extra material—10 or 15 percent is common—for waste, damage, or cutting mistakes, and you're on your way.

Measure twice, cut once

Just what tools and skills do you need to build a fence? Actually, it's pretty basic. Toolwise, you could probably make do with a tape measure, a level, a saw, and a hammer. For a complete rundown, see "Tools of the Trade," on the facing page.

The required building skills are also basic. You'll need to plot layout lines; measure level; and cut posts, rails, and boards. The photos below outline these tasks. Some fence

PLAY IT SAFE

Always follow safe working practices. Wear eye protection when using a striking tool such as a hammer, work gloves for handling rough lumber or sharp objects, and a dust mask or respirator when you may be inhaling dust or harmful products (when cutting pressure-treated lumber, for instance). When working with power tools, follow the manufacturer's operating instructions and wear hearing protection.

designs—post-and-rail, picket, and lath, for example—may require more precise joinery or shaping. But even then, there's often a simpler version to be had. If you need further help with tools or techniques, see the Sunset book *Basic Carpentry.*

BASIC FENCE-BUILDING SKILLS

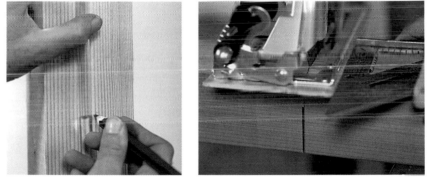

When measuring (above left), pull the tape taut, then draw a "V" or "crow's foot" that points to the line on the tape.

A water level (center) accurately transfers a set height from one post to another. Have a helper align the water height on one post; mark the corresponding water level on the second post.

To cut thick 4-by-4 posts with a circular saw (above right), first make one pass with the saw set at maximum depth; then flip the piece over and make a second pass. A square or guide helps keep the saw base on line.

Decorative board tops, or "dog ears," are easily cut with a crosscut saw (left) or a jigsaw. Mark cutting lines with a square and pencil; then saw on the outer or "waste" side of each line.

LAYING OUT THE FENCE LINE

The first step in building your fence is to locate the exact course it will take and mark that line with stakes and mason's twine. If you're building the fence on or right next to a boundary or property line, you must be certain exactly where that line is located. If you're not building a boundary fence, simply measure out the desired length of the fence line and mark the location of end posts, as outlined below. We also show you how to mark corners and how to plot hillside fences.

PLOTTING A STRAIGHT FENCE

1 Lay out the fence run
Measure the fence run and drive a stake to mark each end post (above left). Then run mason's twine or string between the stakes, drawing it tight and tying it firmly at each end (above right).

2 Mark intermediate posts
Locate intermediate posts by measuring along the twine and marking their centers with tape or chalk. Use a plumb bob to locate the center of each post, then mark the spot temporarily with a nail and a piece of paper, as shown at right.

LAYING OUT A STRAIGHT FENCE. To plot a straight run, lay out the desired length and direction of the fence line and mark each end with a solidly driven stake. Stretch mason's twine or string tightly between the stakes. Ideally, the twine should be as close to the ground as possible, but if bushes or other obstructions are in the way, use tall stakes so the twine can be attached high enough to clear them.

To mark the position of intermediate posts, measure along the twine and mark post centers on it. Using a plumb bob or level, transfer each mark to the ground, as shown in the photo below.

PLOTTING A RIGHT-ANGLE CORNER. If your fence calls for an exact 90-degree corner, use the "3-4-5" measuring method shown at the top of the facing page. Set up the first fence line as described for a straight fence. Then plot the corner by stringing a second line roughly perpendicular to the first and establishing the angle as pictured, pulling the twine taut and carefully driving a stake to anchor it.

PLOTTING HILLSIDE FENCING. If you've planned a fence for a hillside with a steep or bumpy slope, it's best to have a professional lay out and build the fence. But if the slope is fairly gradual and uniform (no big humps or depressions along the fence line), you can plot it yourself, using one of the methods shown at right.

PLOTTING A RIGHT ANGLE

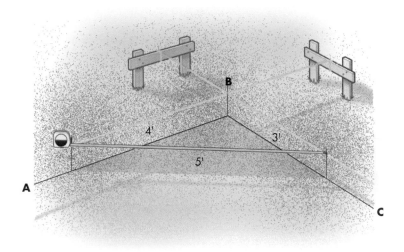

Set up the first fence line (point A to point B) as described on the facing page, then stretch another length of twine roughly perpendicular to it. On line AB, mark the twine 4 feet from point B; then mark the second line (BC) 3 feet from point B.

Adjust line BC until the diagonal measurement between the two marks is 5 feet, as shown at left.

FOLLOWING A SLOPE

To plot contour fencing, drive your end stakes and stretch twine between them; the twine should be high enough to clear any bumpy ground between the stakes.

Measure and mark the intermediate post spans along the string. Then use a plumb bob to transfer the marks to the ground below.

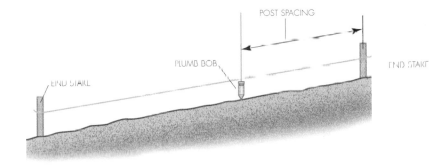

DESCENDING IN STEPS

Drive end stakes, using a tall stake at the downhill end so that its top is at about the same elevation as the uphill end stake. Use a water level to transfer a level mark from uphill stake to downhill stake, then string mason's twine between these points as shown.

Measure the fence's run along the level line, then divide this length by the number of posts you plan in order to arrive at even post spacings. To figure the drop in each step, simply divide the total drop by the number of spacings.

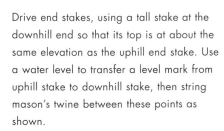

SETTING POSTS

Installing posts is the most important part of fence building. Posts that aren't set firmly in the ground will be the bane of an otherwise solidly built fence. They must be plumb in their holes and perfectly lined up, too, or you'll run into trouble when adding rails and siding materials.

The post-setting process can be divided into three steps: digging the postholes, setting the posts, and aligning the posts. Setting and aligning posts is best done by two people—one to hold and align each post while the other fills the hole with concrete or earth and gravel.

Some fence designs call for post tops to be precisely level with one another. These include fences with rails attached to the post tops and fences with rails recessed into the posts by means of a dado or mortise. You can either cut the posts before setting them—which means you'll need to set all the posts to exactly the same height—or you can set the posts first and then cut them in place. If you choose the second option, making the cuts is trickier.

Posts are generally set in concrete, but if the soil is stable (not subject to sliding, cracking, or frost-heaving), earth-and-gravel fill is adequate for lightweight fences such as lattice, picket, and some post-and-board types no taller than 4 feet. For an overview of both techniques, see the drawings on the facing page. After setting posts in fresh concrete, you have about 20 minutes to align them before the concrete hardens. Let cure for two days.

SETTING POSTS IN CONCRETE

1 Dig postholes

Using a posthole digger or auger, dig holes 6 inches deeper than the posts will go and 2½ to 3 times the post diameter. For maximum strength, undercut postholes slightly so that they are slightly wider at the bottom than at the top.

2 Set end posts in concrete

Place a flat stone in the bottom of each hole as a platform for the post; add 4 to 6 inches of gravel. Center the post in the hole and shovel in concrete, tamping it down with a broomstick or capped steel pipe. Use a level to adjust the post plumb. Continue filling until the concrete extends 1 to 2 inches above ground level, then slope it away from the post to divert water.

POSTHOLE PROFILES

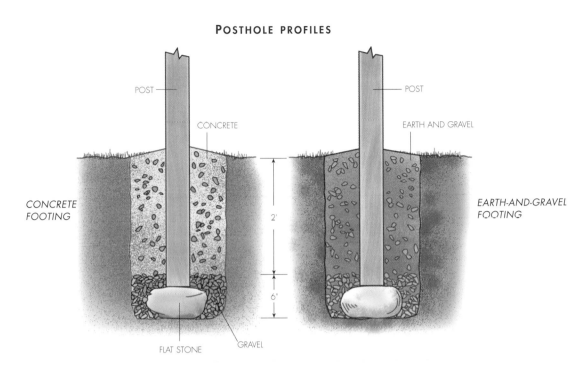

POST

CONCRETE

EARTH AND GRAVEL

POST

CONCRETE
FOOTING

EARTH-AND-GRAVEL
FOOTING

2'

6"

FLAT STONE   GRAVEL

4 Align the posts

Position two end or corner posts so their faces are parallel, (see step 3). Then use spacer blocks and mason's twine to locate line posts, spacing each a block's thickness from the line.

3 Brace posts

To hold posts while concrete sets, make up braces from lengths of 1 x 4s and short stakes. Drive the stakes into the ground and attach the braces with one nail or screw each so they can be pivoted; then fasten braces to two adjacent sides of the post.

5 Adjust post heights

To cut posts after they're set, first use a water level or mason's twine and line level to mark the heights. Then use a reciprocating saw or handsaw to make the cuts. Take your time, and aim for a nice, straight cut.

ADDING RAILS

Once the fence posts are set and aligned, the hardest part of your fence project is behind you. The next step is to attach the rails. If they are not attached firmly and squarely, all of your painstaking work in aligning the fence posts will be wasted.

Rails can be butted between the posts, lapped across the tops or sides of the posts, or inset (dadoed) flush with the face of the posts.

Posts set in concrete should be left for at least two days before you attach rails and siding. You may need to treat or prime cut rail ends before attaching them (see "Fence Finishes" on page 125).

BUTTED RAILS. Cut the rails to fit snugly between the posts and attach them with fence-rail or angle brackets (see photo below right) or by "toenailing" them (nailing from the top or bottom rail edge at an angle into the post, as shown on the facing page). If you toenail rails, it's easiest if you first nail 2-by-4 cleats to the post to help support the rails. Make sure rails are aligned and level before fastening them.

LAPPED RAILS. Most often used with vertical board fences, lapped rails are the easiest kind to install. Simply lap the rails across post tops or sides, making sure they're long enough to span at least three posts.

Level the rails and nail them to the posts with common or box nails. If rails are lapped on post tops and meet at a corner, miter the ends. If rails meet at an intermediate post, butt the ends at the middle of the post.

INSET RAILS. Dadoes are square-shouldered notches cut across a post to house a rail; make the dado exactly the dimension of the rail it holds. It's not as tricky as it seems—for a straightforward technique, see "Notching for Rails" on the facing page.

Post-and-rail fences often call for rails that pass through mortises in the posts. For a closer look at both rail fences and mortising, see pages 76–77.

ATTACHING THE RAILS

1 Check for square
With a helper holding the rail level at the other end, use a square to make sure each rail is perpendicular to the posts.

2 Fasten to the posts
Toenail the rail to the posts, or use angle brackets or fence-rail brackets, as shown above.

FIVE RAIL CONNECTIONS

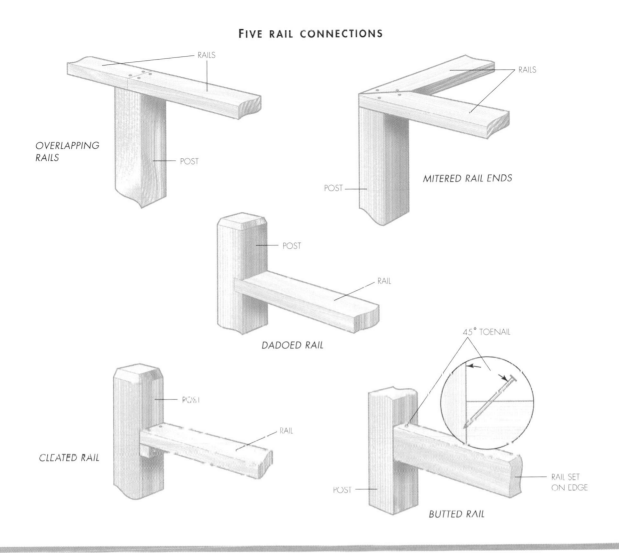

OVERLAPPING RAILS

RAILS

POST

MITERED RAIL ENDS

RAILS

POST

POST

RAIL

DADOED RAIL

POST

RAIL

CLEATED RAIL

45° TOENAIL

POST

RAIL SET ON EDGE

BUTTED RAIL

NOTCHING FOR RAILS

You can recess rails into posts by cutting dadoes into the posts, creating a stronger and more stylish joint than if the pieces are simply butted together.

You'll probably find that it's easier to cut dadoes before the posts are set—but you'll then have to set all the posts at exactly the same height. When you mark cutting lines on the posts, always measure down from the top of the post for both top and bottom rail positions.

Cut the dadoes with a portable circular saw and chisel, as shown at right.

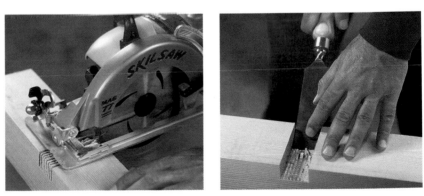

Cutting post dadoes is a two-step process. First, set a circular saw for the depth of the dado, and make multiple cuts (above left) until the wood nearly falls out. Then use a sharp chisel to clean out the waste (above right).

building basics

ATTACHING SIDING

Adding board siding is usually the easiest part of building a fence, but don't jump in before you check to see that your framework is just right. If it isn't, the siding will make any problem all too apparent.

Though there are several ways to attach board siding to a frame, the simplest method is to nail or screw vertical boards to the top and bottom rails. Grapestakes, louvers, basketweave, and many other siding types are applied in much the same way; six of these board-fence cousins are shown on the facing page.

If your fence design includes an optional kickboard, that goes on before the siding boards.

APPLYING BOARD SIDING

1 Align the first board

Cut siding boards to length; then stretch a level line from post to post to mark the bottom of the siding. Check the first board for plumb, then secure it to rails with screws or nails roughly three times as long as the board's thickness.

2 Add additional boards

Secure additional boards one by one, checking alignment as you go. If boards are spaced a few inches apart, rip a spacer (see page 75) to the appropriate width and use that to keep the boards aligned.

INSTALLING A KICKBOARD. You can attach a kickboard to the front of the posts or center it under the bottom rail. Both designs are shown at right. Attaching the kickboard to the posts provides a ledge on which to set the siding. Center the kickboard under the bottom rail when you want the fence to look the same on both sides.

Unless the kickboard will rest right on the ground, dig a narrow trench, 4 to 6 inches deep, between the posts. This allows boards to be set into the ground visually while avoiding actual contact with the soil.

KICKBOARD DETAILS

KICKBOARD

1 × 1 CLEATS

KICKBOARD

INSTALLING VERTICAL BOARD SIDING. To keep siding at an even height, make sure all the boards are exactly the same length. Precut any top spikes or "dog ears" (see page 104).

Then stretch mason's twine taut along the fence to mark the desired lower edge of the siding; check the line with a level. Align the bottom of each board with this line. Alternatively, you can nail a board to the posts to serve as a temporary guide.

Use a level to check each board for plumb before fastening it. Leave a slight gap between boards, since they'll expand and contract with weather changes.

The number of nails or screws you need depends on the width of the boards; use the guidelines below.

Lumber width (nominal)	Nails needed across width
2"	1
3"–6"	2
8"	3

SIX BOARD-FENCE ALTERNATIVES

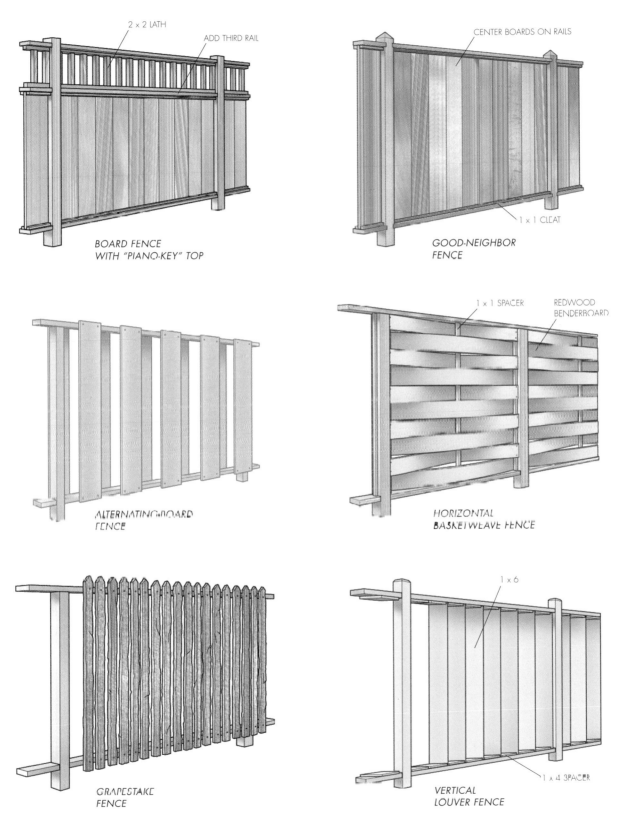

2 × 2 LATH

ADD THIRD RAIL

BOARD FENCE
WITH "PIANO-KEY" TOP

CENTER BOARDS ON RAILS

1 × 1 CLEAT

GOOD-NEIGHBOR
FENCE

ALTERNATING-BOARD
FENCE

1 × 1 SPACER

REDWOOD
BENDERBOARD

HORIZONTAL
BASKETWEAVE FENCE

GRAPESTAKE
FENCE

1 × 6

1 × 4 SPACER

VERTICAL
LOUVER FENCE

PICKET FENCES

Traditionally, the picket fence has been associated with Colonial American architecture, but today it's found with almost any type of house, whether in the city or the country. The wide range of picket and post top patterns available allows an individual touch while staying within the boundaries of traditional design. A gallery of treatments is shown below.

PICKET FENCE COMPONENTS

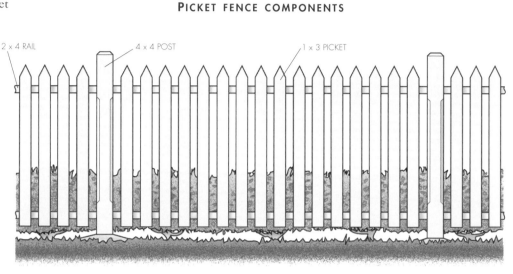

2 x 4 RAIL   4 x 4 POST   1 x 3 PICKET

The typical picket fence is about 3 feet high, with 4 by 4 posts on 6-foot centers and 2 by 4 rails butted between them. Overall post length is 5 feet (3 feet above ground and 2 feet below). Pickets are most often 1 by 3s spaced 2½ inches apart, but many other sizes and spacings are used as well.

Lumber dealers and home centers don't always carry ready-made pickets—and those that do may offer just a few designs. If you can't find what you want, you can cut the patterns yourself (see the facing page) or have a cabinet shop or woodworker do the work.

For decorative post tops, you'll probably want to have any complex design cut by an experienced woodworker rather than doing it yourself. Simpler yet, look for prefabricated post caps and finials—for a sampling, see page 113.

Once pickets and posts are shaped, install the posts as described on pages 68–69. Butt the rails between posts and add a kickboard, if you wish. Then install the pickets using a spacer slat, as shown at right.

PICKET PATTERNS

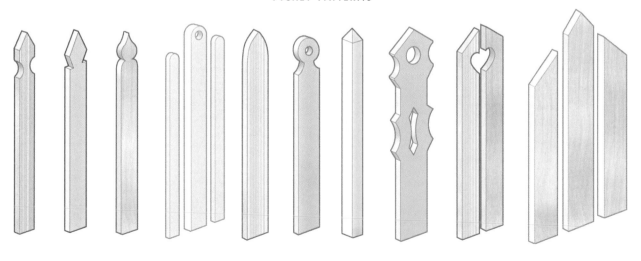

CUSTOM–CUTTING PICKETS

Use a handsaw or jigsaw to cut simple pointed pickets; the jigsaw (shown below) also shapes more intricate designs. Make a "master pattern" first, then trace it on the boards to be cut.

To save work, clamp several boards together and cut them together, as shown. A power drill and hole saw can make circular cutouts.

Spacing the pickets

To ensure uniform height and spacing of successive pickets, make a spacer slat as shown above. Cut the slat to the exact length of the pickets and attach a small cleat to the back so that, when it's hung on the top rail, the slat will be at an even height with the pickets.

Position the spacer alongside the first picket, then place the next picket against it. Align the bottoms of the picket and slat; nail or screw the picket to the top and bottom rails. Remove the slat and repeat the process.

POST-TOP PROFILES

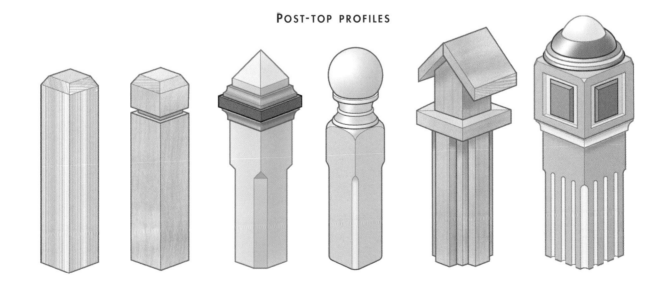

RAIL FENCES

Homesteaders originally built split rail fences in a zigzag pattern, stacking rails on top of each other and supporting the bottom on rocks. (An example is shown on page 7.) As trees became scarcer and property lines more precise, fence-builders straightened out the zigzag pattern by stacking rails between paired posts. These double post-and-rail fences still required a fair amount of wood, and eventually people began to build fences with fewer rails, mortising them into single posts.

Post-and-board fences are even simpler, using modern dimension lumber to create a similar effect.

THE POST-AND-RAIL FENCE. There are a number of ways to mortise rails into posts, depending on the relative sizes and shapes of the posts and rails. One of the most common methods is shown below—overlapping the rails and cutting tenons into the rail ends. The fence shown features 6-foot-long rectangular posts, roughly 5 inches by 6 inches thick, The split rails shown are roughly 3 inches by 4 inches thick and about 6 to 8 feet long.

A more formal look can be achieved with a post-and-rail fence by using dimension lumber—standard 4-by-4 rails set between 4-by-4 posts, as shown below right. You can dado the rails into the posts (as shown), mortise them, or just butt them between posts. For a variation, rotate the rails 45 degrees and toenail them between the posts.

THE POST-AND-BOARD FENCE. Familiar sights along country roads, post-and-board fences have traditionally been used to enclose large acreages. Among the easiest fences to build, these use perhaps the least amount of lumber of any wood fence.

The typical post-and-board fence is 3 to 4 feet high and has three rails, usually 1 by 4s or 1 by 6s, attached to the sides of the posts and running parallel to the ground.

But post-and-board fences accommodate a number of design variations, like those shown on the facing page. Some styles serve purposes beyond simply adding visual interest; taller versions (4 to 6 feet tall) are used for containing livestock and for horse corrals. Sturdier designs such as those used to pen livestock may have 2-by-6 rails. Lower versions (2½ to 4 feet tall) are often seen in front of ranch-style houses or country estates. Post-and-board fences adapt especially well to hillsides and rolling terrain.

POST-AND-RAIL FENCES

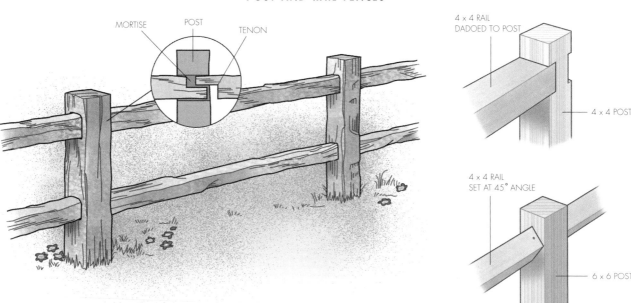

MORTISE　　POST　　TENON

4 x 4 RAIL DADOED TO POST

4 x 4 POST

4 x 4 RAIL SET AT 45° ANGLE

6 x 6 POST

MORTISING A POST

On signature post-and-rail fences, the rails are passed through mortises (holes) cut through the posts. Split posts with precut mortises may be available; if not, you can make your own. Mortises are best cut before the posts are set in place.

To make the mortises, lay the post across two sawhorses, then mark each mortise and cut it as shown below. Matching tenons (mortise-shaped tabs), required unless mortises accommodate the entire rail end, are best cut with a sharp handsaw or power circular saw.

To make a mortise, drill 1-inch holes (near right) through the post, then use a chisel (far right) to clear the waste and square up the mortise.

POST-AND-BOARD FENCES

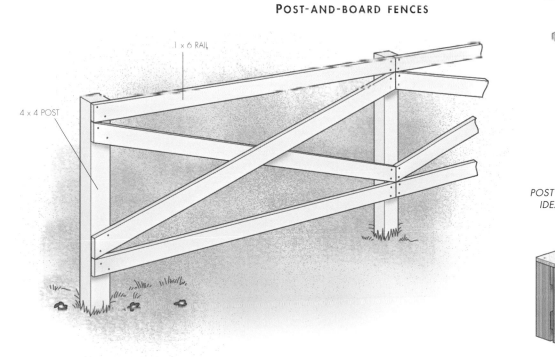

1 x 6 RAIL

4 x 4 POST

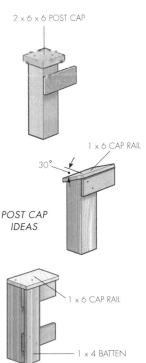

2 x 6 x 6 POST CAP

1 x 6 CAP RAIL

30°

POST CAP IDEAS

1 x 6 CAP RAIL

1 x 4 BATTEN

LATH & LATTICE

Lath and lattice screens and fences are light, lacy structures, originally associated with Victorian architecture. A tightly woven lattice can help screen out an objectionable view while allowing air and light into the yard; widely spaced lath can preserve a view, serve as a traffic director, or provide a backdrop for tall plantings. Because of their light weight and open design, lattice fences and screens can be built without unduly heavy framing members or bracing.

The screen shown below uses preassembled lattice panels. The posts are 4 by 4s, 8 feet long and set 2 feet in the ground, 4 feet on center. The rails are 2 by 4s cut to length to butt between the posts. Use 1-by-1 cleats, as shown, to secure lattice to both posts and rails. Once the lattice is attached, add a 2-by-6 cap atop the posts.

Thicker, more robust lath can float atop an open frame or solid fence, doubling as a bold graphic and a trellis for climbing plants. Build the crisscross pattern directly atop the frame, or build it on the ground (as shown at right) and then fix it to a fence.

Assembling lath

Lay out lath with a tape measure, then tack it together on the back side of each intersection. Waterproof glue helps secure the joints.

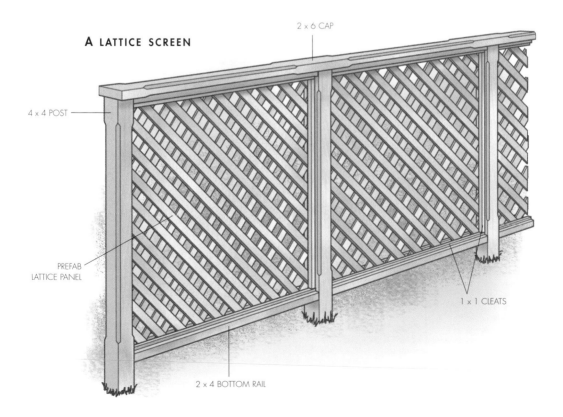

A LATTICE SCREEN

2 x 6 CAP

4 x 4 POST

PREFAB LATTICE PANEL

1 x 1 CLEATS

2 x 4 BOTTOM RAIL

WIRE FENCING

Wire mesh has numerous applications in fencing. Heavy mesh provides security and offers support for plants without completely blocking a view. Chain-link fencing is handy for everyday enclosures. Prefabricated vinyl and steel fences (pages 110–111) are modern, modular successors to traditional wrought iron.

The fence shown at right consists of welded wire mesh (see page 108) attached to a simple wood frame of 4-by-4 posts and 2-by-4 rails. The mesh comes in widths from 3 to 6 feet. The fence we show uses the 4-foot width, but you can adapt the design to a 3- or 6-foot fence; you might also want to substitute a tighter mesh.

Fasten framing members with nails three times as long as the thickness of the wood. Use ³/₄-inch galvanized staples to hold the wire to the posts and rails. Cut the mesh, as required, with wire cutters; where two panels join, overlap them as shown at right. If you like, add a kickboard below and additional wood framing atop the wire mesh.

A WOOD-AND-WIRE FENCE

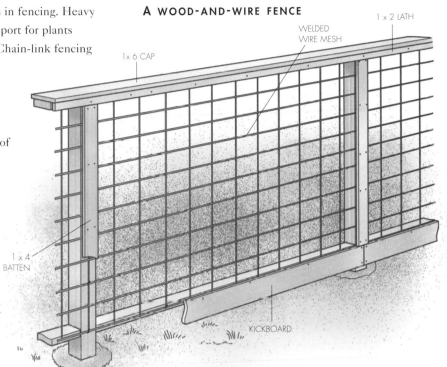

1 x 2 LATH
WELDED WIRE MESH
1 x 6 CAP
1 x 4 BATTEN
KICKBOARD

GALVANIZED STAPLES

Secure it with staples

Fasten welded wire mesh to fence posts and rails with ³/₄-inch galvanized staples. Where two wire pieces are joined, overlap one row of wire rectangles and join the pieces with staples, as shown at right.

BUILDING A MASONRY WALL

BUILDING WITH masonry units can be strenuous work. But as masons have found throughout history, a careful and methodical approach begets good results. TAKE YOUR TIME, exploring the various designs and patterns available to you. The guidelines that follow are for short walls—those up to about 3 feet. FOR ANYTHING HIGHER you'll probably need extra reinforcing, and a permit and/or engineer's report may be required. Be sure to check with your building department for local requirements.

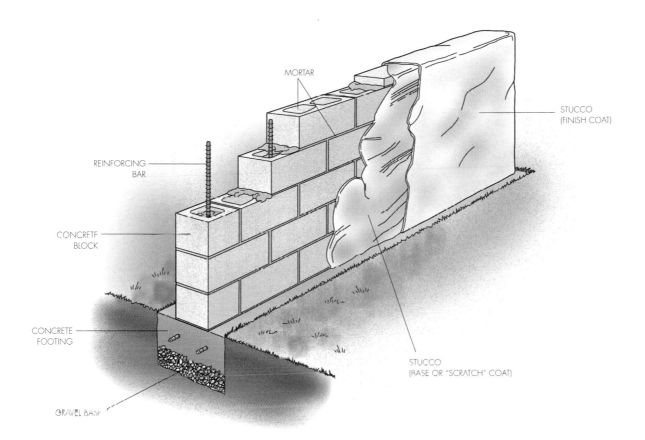

MORTAR

REINFORCING
BAR

CONCRETE
BLOCK

CONCRETE
FOOTING

GRAVEL BASE

STUCCO
(FINISH COAT)

STUCCO
(BASE OR "SCRATCH" COAT)

The basic building blocks

Suitable materials for garden walls include the many kinds
of brick, concrete block, and stone. You'll find instructions
for working with each of these on the following pages; for
more about materials, refer to "A Shopper's Guide," beginning on page 101. Besides the bricks, blocks, or rocks,
you'll also need to make the acquaintance of a few other
wall components, as shown above.

Except for very low walls (no more than 12 inches high)
or dry-stacked stone, you'll need a solid concrete founda-
tion, or *footing*. The procedure for pouring a footing is
detailed on page 83. Footings are usually twice the width
of the wall and at least as deep as the wall is wide—but
consult local codes for exceptions. Add 6 inches to allow for
a gravel base. In cold-weather areas, you may need to
extend footings deeper to make sure they are below the
frost line.

Mortar is the bonding agent that holds masonry units
together. It also seals out wind and water, compensates for
variations in the size of masonry units, and provides
decorative effects, depending on how the joints are tooled.
For details on mixing mortar, see page 85.

In most cases, a freestanding wall more than 2 or 3 feet
high should have some kind of *reinforcement* to tie its different portions together and keep it from buckling. Before
you proceed too far in your planning, check on requirements with your local building department.

Steel reinforcing bar, or rebar, can provide either
horizontal or vertical stiffening. Laid horizontally with the
mortar for the length of a wall, steel helps tie wall sections
together. Placed vertically (between double rows of brick,
for example, or in the hollow cores of concrete block), rebar
adds strength that can keep a wall from toppling under its
own weight.

TOOLS OF THE TRADE: MASONRY

To join the home mason's ranks, you'll need a few tools. A quick search of your workshop or garage may turn up a good number of them: a hammer, a saw, a 2-foot carpenter's level, a square, a steel measuring tape, and a shovel.

Some additional tools will make the job go smoothly. Mason's twine is useful for laying out perimeter lines or guides for straight courses; corner blocks help hold the lines in place. A small line level and a 4-foot mason's level are helpful for checking over a large area.

A brick set or a broad-bladed cold chisel can be used for cutting and dressing bricks. Drive it with a hand sledge. For most jobs involving mortar, you'll need a pointed trowel with a 10-inch blade. For concrete surfacing, use a wooden float and/or a steel trowel. To mix mortar, consider a mortar hoe.

You may want to invest in some optional paraphernalia: a couple of jointers to shape mortar joints; a mason's hammer to chip rough edges away from a cut brick, block, or stone; and a hand set or other thin-bladed chisel to shape and split stone.

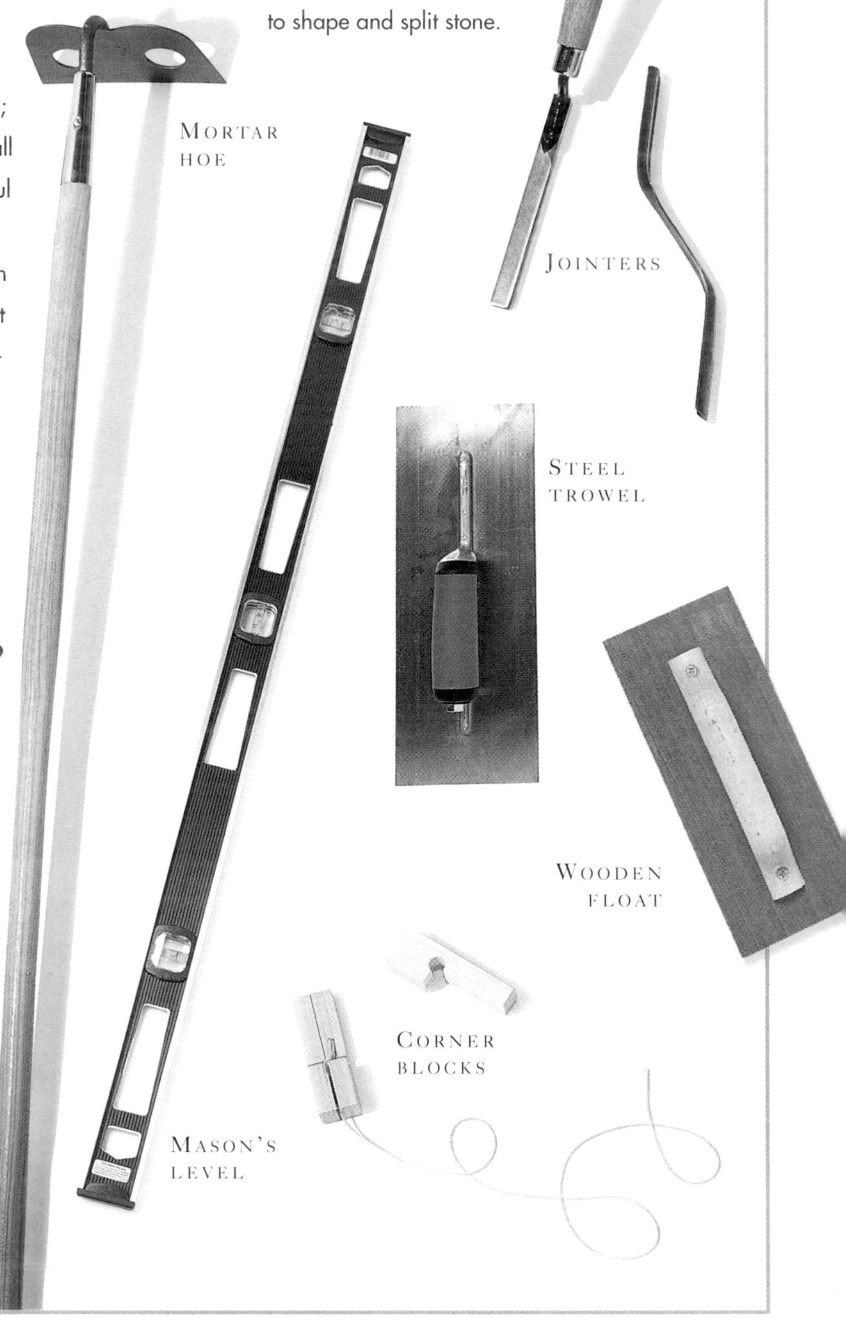

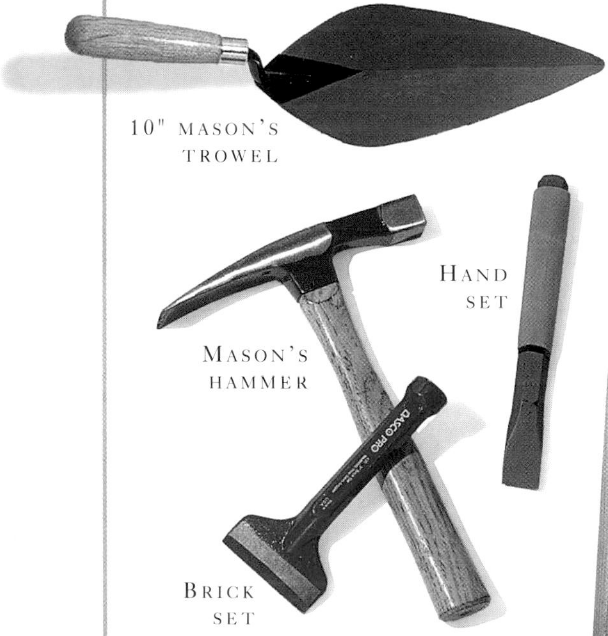

MORTAR
HOE

JOINTERS

STEEL
TROWEL

10" MASON'S
TROWEL

WOODEN
FLOAT

HAND
SET

MASON'S
HAMMER

CORNER
BLOCKS

BRICK
SET

MASON'S
LEVEL

Pouring a footing

Except for a dry stone wall, it's best to use concrete for the footing of a masonry wall. Unless local building codes call for something different, plan to lay your footing on a 6-inch-deep gravel bed dug deep enough that the bottom of the footing sits below the frost line for your area. You may need to add reinforcement to the footing, usually reinforcing bar; check with your building department.

Lay out the entire length of the wall, marking corners with stakes. Outline a trench the size of the desired footing by driving stakes at each corner and stretching mason's twine level between them. As you dig, these lines will serve as a reference for checking depth.

Dig a straight-sided trench, level the bottom, and tamp it firmly. Build 2-by-4 forms, as shown at right. Stepped forms, which descend like stairs, allow you to manage sloped lots.

Shovel in gravel for the base, making sure all the gravel is below the frost line. Then mix the concrete as outlined on page 117 and pour it directly into the form, tamping it with a shovel as you pour. Use a piece of wood as a screed to make the surface level. Before the concrete completely hardens, insert any vertical reinforcing bars you're using.

Cover the concrete with a plastic sheet and let it cure for two days. Then you can remove the forms and start working on the wall itself.

For more information on both concrete and formwork, see the Sunset title *Complete Masonry Book*.

BUILDING A CONCRETE FOOTING

1 Dig a trench
Drive stakes and string mason's twine level to outline the top of the footing. Dig a trench for the footing, then level and tamp the bottom.

2 Build the forms
Construct concrete forms from 2-by lumber and stakes. Add a 6-inch layer of gravel. Set horizontal reinforcing bars, if used, atop broken bricks or other rubble.

3 Pour the concrete
Mix concrete, distribute it inside the trench, and use a board as a screed to smooth it level with the form tops. Insert any vertical reinforcing that's required.

PLAY IT SAFE

Masonry work requires some basic safety strategy. Portland cement is irritating to the eyes, nose, and mouth; when you work with it, wear a dust mask and goggles. Wet mortar and concrete are caustic to the skin; wear gloves and tuck your sleeves into them.

Don safety goggles or glasses before cutting any masonry units. And always bend your knees, not your back, when lifting heavy stones or blocks.

BUILDING A BRICK WALL

Building with brick is pleasant work. The units are sized for easy one-hand lifting, and bricklaying takes on a certain rhythm once you get the hang of it. As with all masonry projects, attention to detail is the key.

Your brick wall requires a sturdy concrete footing; for instructions, see page 83. The footing needs to cure for about two days.

When you're ready to start the wall, distribute your bricks alongside the footing. Unless they're already damp, hose them down several hours before you begin work.

BRICK PATTERNS. Over the years, many brick bonding patterns have evolved. *Headers* (bricks running perpendicular to the wall's length) and *stretchers* (bricks running lengthwise along the wall) have been used in a variety of combinations in each layer—called a "course" or "wythe" —in a brick wall.

In addition to the common (or American) bond, which uses headers for every fifth course, three other patterns are often used for garden walls. English bond alternates courses of stretchers and headers, forming very strong brick walls. Flemish bond alternates headers and stretchers within each course. Running bond simply staggers rows of stretchers; use it for low walls or brick veneer only.

WHAT ABOUT REINFORCING? Brick walls more than about 2 feet high need reinforcing. What's required may be as simple as a cap of header bricks or as exacting as engineered steel reinforcing. For higher freestanding walls, you have two choices: one is wider brick pilasters, or columns, built as part of the wall; the other is steel reinforcing. To make an informed choice that's consistent with codes, check with your local building department.

FINISHING MORTAR JOINTS. Finishing—or "striking"—mortar joints compacts the mortar and shapes it to shed water. Finishing is an important part of masonry because it contributes to the strength and weather-tightness of the

Continued on page 86

FOUR BRICK PATTERNS

HEADER
COURSE

COMMON
(AMERICAN) BOND

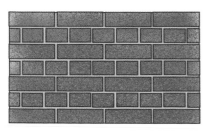

ENGLISH BOND

FLEMISH BOND

RUNNING BOND

WORKING WITH MORTAR

If your plans call for masonry walls, chances are you'll be adding mortaring to your do-it-yourself resume. Here's a quick course to get you started.

Mortar proportions vary with the intended use, but the ingredients stay the same: cement, lime, sand, and water. You can make your own mortar (see page 117) or buy more expensive ready-mix by the bag at building supply stores.

Mix it well

Small amounts of mortar can easily be mixed by hand. You'll need a wheelbarrow or other container and a hoe or shovel. To make your own mortar, mix the sand, cement, and lime into a pile with the hoe, form a hole in the top, and add some water; mix, then repeat. Mix only enough to last about two hours; more than that is likely to end up being wasted.

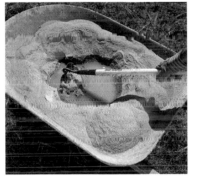

A wheelbarrow (above) is ideal for mixing mortar. Blend dry ingredients, then form a hole and fill it with water. Hoe dry ingredients toward the center to blend.

Ready for use, mortar should have a smooth, granular consistency; it should spread well and adhere to vertical surfaces but not smear the face of the work. Add water a little at a time until these conditions are met.

If your job is large, you may wish to rent a power mixer.

Throwing a mortar line

For bricks and other similar-size masonry units, you'll need to learn to throw a mortar line—an even bed of mortar several units long. Here's how the pros do it.

Place one or two shovelfuls of mortar on a mortar bed; a piece of plywood about 2 feet square will do. Load your trowel (a 10-inch trowel holds the right amount for brick-work) by slicing off a wedge of mortar and scooping it up. Give the trowel a shake to dislodge the excess.

Now comes the tricky part—throwing the line. As you bring your arm back toward your body, you rotate the trowel, depositing mortar in an even line about 1 inch thick, 1 brick wide, and 4 or 5 bricks long. Throwing a neat mortar line takes practice, so try it out before starting your wall.

Once the line is thrown, furrow it with the point of the trowel as shown below. The furrow ensures that the bricks are bedded evenly and causes excess mortar to be squeezed out to either side as the bricks are laid.

Using a pointed trowel, throw, then furrow a mortar line that's several bricks long, as shown above. "Butter" brick ends as shown at left.

completed project. Various joint styles are pictured on the facing page; if you live in a freezing or rainy climate, use a concave or weathered joint.

Finishing tools vary, depending on the type of joint desired. Special tools are available, or you can use a trowel, a piece of wood, or a steel rod.

Joints should be finished when the mortar is neither so soft that it smears the wall nor so hard that the tool shapes it with difficulty and leaves black marks. The mortar is

ready to finish when it's "thumbprint hard"—when pressing on it leaves a slight indentation.

Once joints are finished and mortar is well set, clean away excess mortar by brushing the wall with a stiff brush. If mortar smears onto the bricks, you may be able to wipe it off with a damp sponge, but take care not to get the joints too wet or you will weaken them. Alternatively, wait a day and then clean with a mild solution of muriatic acid (available where masonry materials are sold).

BUILDING A BRICK WALL

1 Lay a dry run
Mark the outer edges of the wall on the footing with chalk. Lay a single "dry" course of bricks with 1/2-inch joint spaces along the length of the wall. (Dowels help set even spacings.) Mark joints with pencil lines on the footing.

2 Lay the first bricks
Remove the dry-laid bricks. Spread mortar on the footing and lay the first brick. Apply mortar to one end of the second and third bricks and set them in place. Check that bricks are level. Lay the backup course the same way.

4 Build a lead
Continue laying stretchers until the lead (wall end) is 7 or 8 bricks high, looking like stairsteps; use a level to check your work as you go. Now build the lead at the other end of the wall.

5 Fill in between leads
Stretch mason's twine between leads as a guide, keeping it about 1/16 inch away from the bricks. Lay bricks from the ends toward the center, course by course. Apply mortar to both ends of the closure bricks and insert them straight down.

SIX MORTAR
JOINTS

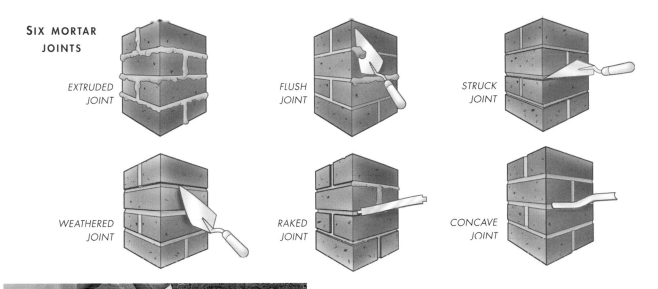

EXTRUDED
JOINT

FLUSH
JOINT

STRUCK
JOINT

WEATHERED
JOINT

RAKED
JOINT

CONCAVE
JOINT

3 Lay a header course

Cut two bricks to three-quarter length to begin the second, or header, course; mortar in place. Lay four headers across the width of the wall, applying mortar as before.

6 Strike the joints

Every 10 minutes or so—depending on the weather—stop and strike the mortar joints. Using the tool of your choice, smooth all horizontal joints first, then smooth the vertical or head joints.

CUTTING BRICKS

No matter how carefully you plan, some cutting is almost inevitable.

For just a few cuts, the handiest tool is a chisel-like implement called a brick set. Lay the brick on flat sand and place the chisel on the cut line, its bevel facing away from the part of the brick to be used (top right). Tap the chisel with a hand sledge or soft-headed hammer (wear safety glasses). For cleanest results, tap lightly to score a groove on all four sides of the brick before administering the final blow. If necessary, chip away rough edges with the brick set or a mason's hammer.

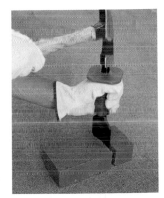

If you have a lot of cutting to do, a diamond-bladed wet saw is your best bet (bottom right). Rent one for the day from a masonry supplier or tool rental outlet.

BUILDING WITH CONCRETE BLOCKS

Laying concrete block is like building with brick (see pages 84-87), but it goes much faster. Blocks are available in several shapes and sizes (see pages 114-115). Though some decorative walls stand on their own merits, standard blocks, set in a traditional mortar bed, are usually the backbone for a more decorative veneer (see page 91).

New interlocking blocks are strong enough to simply be stacked and left alone, but surface bonding mortar adds strength, as well as an attractive stucco surface. Stackable retaining blocks are a do-it-yourselfer's dream: use them to make no-fuss garden borders or retaining walls, curved or straight.

INTERLOCKING BLOCKS. To build the recommended footing for a standard block wall, follow the directions on page 83. Plan the positioning of blocks by fitting a dry course on the cured footing; mark the wall's perimeter, then set the blocks aside. If the exact length of the wall is not critical, plan to use all full- and half-sized blocks, so you don't have to cut any. Use a solid-faced block wherever the block end will be exposed.

Mix a batch of surface-bonding mortar, made for this specific purpose. Then follow the steps shown on the facing page.

Plan to top your wall with a course of solid cap blocks. For extra strength, you can fill the blocks' hollow cores with steel reinforcing bars and grout (thin, soupy mortar). Check with local building authorities about the best plan of attack.

Finally, coat the wall with a ¼-inch layer of surface-bonding mortar, cut control joints, and add the texture of your choice, as shown. For additional veneering options, see page 91.

STACKABLE RETAINING BLOCKS. Need a low retaining wall? These stacking, interlocking blocks are one of the few foolproof ways for a do-it-yourselfer to build one. Most interlocking blocks have a lip at the rear bottom that slips over the top back edge of the block below it. Others are anchored via grooves or even fiberglass pins. Either type can be installed without mortar.

Lay out the site, using stakes and mason's twine to plot a straight wall. For a curved wall, plot the line with a garden hose and mark it with sand.

After doing any necessary slope excavating, dig a trench 6 inches wider and 6 inches deeper than the width of your blocks. Fill the trench with compactible gravel and tamp it with a hand tamper or the end of a 4 by 4. For added stability, rent a vibrating plate compactor.

Now it's show time. Set the bottom row of blocks upside down and backwards so the lips face up at the front. Check for level and adjust as needed by adding or removing gravel from underneath. Lay the second and third rows right side up; then fill in behind the blocks as needed with gravel.

Continue stacking and filling until you have laid the blocks that will be second to the top. Using a caulking gun, apply several squiggles of construction adhesive (shown at left); set the top blocks in the adhesive. Spread landscape fabric (available at garden or building centers) on the gravel, and fill in behind the top blocks with soil.

Stackable retaining blocks have interlocking lips that slip over the backs of each course below. The top course, shown above, is secured with adhesive.

BUILDING A SURFACE-BONDED WALL

1 Lay the first course

First lay out the blocks on the footing, mark their outlines, and remove them. Lightly wet the footing, then spread a bed of surface-bonding mortar about ½ inch thick. Set the first course of blocks in the mortar. As you go, use a level to check that the blocks form an even, level surface.

2 Stack the blocks

Once the bottom course is laid, stack the next courses in a running bond pattern (see page 84). If a block feels wobbly, trowel some mortar on the block below, and set the wobbly block back into place. Tap with a hammer and a scrap of wood to settle the block at the same height as its neighbors.

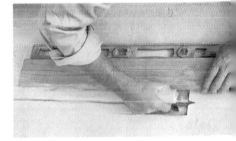

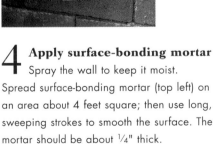

3 Add the cap

For a square-shaped top, cap the wall with interlocking cap blocks. If these are not available, spread surface-bonding mortar on the highest course, and lay solid-faced concrete blocks in the mortar.

4 Apply surface-bonding mortar

Spray the wall to keep it moist. Spread surface-bonding mortar (top left) on an area about 4 feet square; then use long, sweeping strokes to smooth the surface. The mortar should be about ¼" thick.

To control cracking, use a concrete jointer to cut vertical control joints spaced about twice as far apart as the wall's height (top right). Use a straight board as a guide.

Mortar may set up quickly, so be ready to apply the texture of your choice (bottom right). This simple swirl surface is achieved by lightly running the trowel across the surface using sweeping motions of approximately the same radius.

BUILDING A DRY STONE WALL

The key to a successful stone wall is careful fitting. Properly placed stones should appear to be a single unit rather than a pile of rocks. As a rule, you'll want to place stones as they would lie naturally on the ground—not on end or in unnatural positions.

Freestanding, dry-laid stone walls are usually laid in two rough wythes (rows) with rubble fill between them. Bond stones, equivalent to headers in brickwork, run across the wall, tying it together. You should use as many bond stones as possible—at least one for every 10 square feet of wall surface. As you work, be sure that vertical joints are staggered. Keep in mind the stonemason's basic rule: One stone over two, two over one.

STONE WALL DETAILS

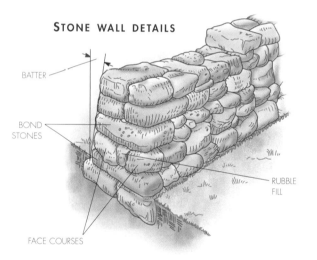

BATTER

BOND STONES

RUBBLE FILL

FACE COURSES

Remove sod and other organic material from an area about 3 inches wider than the desired bottom thickness of the wall. Scrape rather than dig the bottom of the depression so stones will rest on undisturbed soil.

Dry stone walls should slope inward on both surfaces. This tilting of the faces is called "batter" and helps secure the wall, since the faces lean on each other. A good rule of thumb is to plan 3 to 4 inches of batter for each 2 feet of rise. To check your work, make a batter gauge (shown at left) from two scraps of lumber.

BATTER GAUGE

BUILDING A DRY STONE WALL

1 Lay the first stones
Dig a shallow trench about 3 inches wider than the wall's base. Lay a bond stone at either end; then lay stones in two wythes between them. Tightly pack small stones between the wythes to fill in the space.

2 Lay additional courses
Aim to make the courses fairly level. Use your batter gauge to be sure that the wall leans in slightly from front and back. Every third or fourth course, install bond stones every 2 to 3 feet. Fill any large gaps by gently tapping in small stones.

3 Mortar the cap stones
Finish the top with large, flat cap stones that overhang the sides of the wall on either side. For best strength, lay these cap stones in a 1- to 2-inch-thick bed of mortar. The mortar should not be visible.

VENEERING A WALL

You can add texture and color to any wall by covering it with plastering stucco or by facing it with masonry units such as veneering stone. Here's how.

Plaster it

Though plastering is an acquired technique, an accomplished do-it-yourselfer might reasonably tackle a small garden wall.

Plastering a new block wall is a two-part operation. The first layer—or scratch coat—should be about ⅜ inch thick. Before applying the plaster, paint the block with a concrete-bonding agent.

Plastering is a workout. You must trowel the mix onto the surface with enough pressure for it to bond with the block. As the plaster sets, rough it up with a comblike scarifying tool to help the finish coat "bite" (that's why it's called a scratch coat). Let this base coat cure for about two days.

Then apply the finish coat ¼ inch thick, and begin smoothing or "floating" when the sheen has dulled. Use a wooden float, a steel trowel, a sponge, or a stiff brush to give texture to the stucco surface.

Add stone

Applying a stone or brick veneer to an ordinary wall is another good way to dress it up. The resulting wall looks like solid masonry—but it's accomplished with much less labor and expense.

If you're constructing a new wall, first pour the footing, then work on the wall. Use mortar to fix the veneer to the core. Where necessary, use blocks of wood or small rocks to hold the stones in position.

Before the mortar has hardened, go back and fill the joints with mortar. Use a pointed trowel or a mortar bag (below right) to slip mortar into the joints. Wipe the edges with a damp towel, which you will need to clean often.

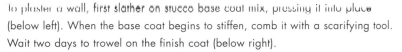
To plaster a wall, first slather on stucco base coat mix, pressing it into place (below left). When the base coat begins to stiffen, comb it with a scarifying tool. Wait two days to trowel on the finish coat (below right).

To face a wall with stone, press rows of stones into a ⅜-inch coat of mortar (top right). If necessary, back-butter the stones with additional mortar. Before the mortar has hardened, go back and fill in the joints (right); then smooth them off.

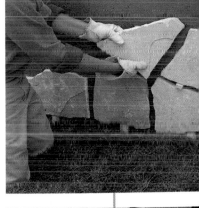

BUILDING A GATE

GATES GET MORE wear and tear than any other part of a fence or wall. To be long-lasting, a gate must be solidly built from dry, straight lumber and attached with heavy-duty hardware. **TO BUILD A BASIC GATE,** you must first set and align gateposts, if they are not already in place. Then you build the gate frame and add the siding; hang the gate; and, finally, install a latch. **WHILE THESE PROCEDURES** are generally straightforward, they do require precise workmanship if the gate is to work smoothly.

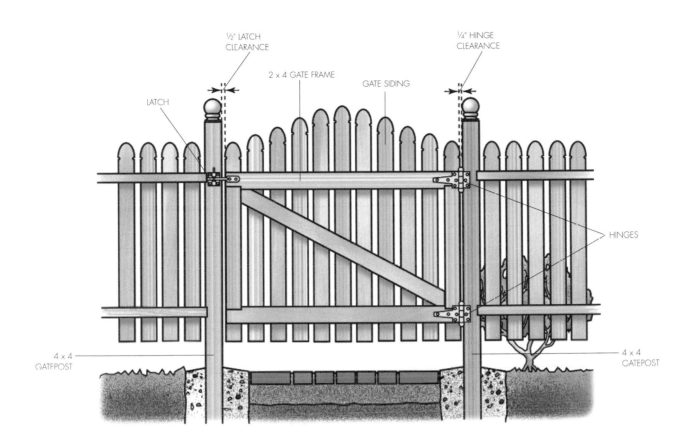

½" LATCH CLEARANCE

¼" HINGE CLEARANCE

2 x 4 GATE FRAME

GATE SIDING

LATCH

HINGES

4 x 4 GATEPOST

4 x 4 GATEPOST

Gate anatomy

The components of a basic gate are illustrated above. Gateposts cut from either 4 by 4 or 6 by 6 lumber define the opening; set parallel and plumb, they're sunk deep into the ground, embedded in concrete.

The standard gate frame is built from dry, straight 2 by 4s with a 2 by 4 diagonal brace. Siding is fastened directly to the frame—we show board siding, but you can use whatever materials match your adjacent fence or wall.

Hinges, latch, and gate stop complete the assembly. Top and bottom hinges are pictured, but it's best to add a third hinge if your gate has heavy siding, is over 5 feet tall, or is more than 3 feet wide. To let your gate swing freely, you'll need to allow for clearance between gateposts and frame on both the hinge and latch sides. You may also need to add a gate stop (page 99) to keep the gate from swinging past its closed position.

Planning pointers

Once you've chosen a gate design, it's time to get specific. Your gate's dimensions will depend on both the height of the fence or wall it serves and the width of the walk, path, or driveway it must span. You'll also need to determine which direction your gate will swing. For gate-planning guidelines, see page 8.

If you're building a new wall or fence, or simply replacing an existing gate, your gateposts may already be in place. Otherwise, you'll need to set them before you build the gate. All gateposts should be set in concrete; sink them into the ground at least ⅓ of their total length.

Using a carpenter's level, check the gateposts, new or old, for plumb. Measure the space between the posts at both the top and the bottom. If it varies by more than ¼ inch, you'll have to compensate by adjusting hinge position, shimming hinges, or adjusting the frame.

BUILDING YOUR GATE

The frame is the skeleton that supports the weight of a gate. A Z-frame (shown at right) is suitable for small openings and lightweight siding such as pickets. The stronger perimeter frame (shown below) is best for most gate designs. Pickets, boards, or other siding materials are fastened directly to either type of frame. The basic steps for building a wood gate are detailed below.

More ornate gates sometimes call for frame-and-panel construction. This technique, based on advanced door joinery, is depicted on page 97. You'll also find several additional gate details there.

BUILDING A FRAME. The step-by-step photo sequence on the facing page shows how to build a basic perimeter gate with a rectangular frame of 2 by 4s and a diagonal 2-by-4 brace. This frame is suitable for gates up to about 6 feet tall and 3 feet wide. Larger gates will require heavier framing members.

Plan the width of the frame to allow clearance space on both hinge and latch sides, as shown on page 93. For gates with standard 2-by-4 framing and 4-by-4 posts, leave ½ inch between the latch post and the gate frame so the gate can swing without rubbing. The clearance space needed on the hinge side will depend on the type of hinges you're using; ¼ inch is sufficient for most standard hinges.

Z-FRAME GATE

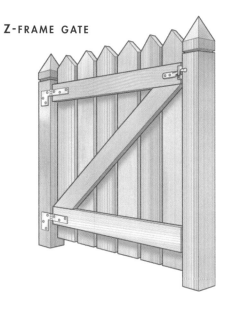

There are two standard ways to brace a perimeter frame. Attaching a board diagonally from the bottom of the hinge side to the top of the latch side, as pictured below left, has the edge in strength as well as looks. Alternatively, a stainless steel cable and turnbuckle assembly run from the bottom of the latch side to the top of the hinge side is a bit easier to install.

TWO PERIMETER FRAMES

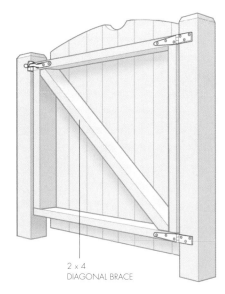

2 x 4
DIAGONAL BRACE

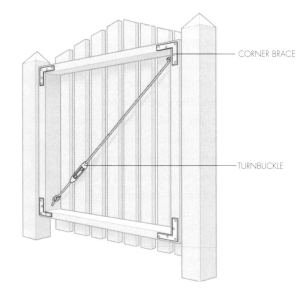

CORNER BRACE

TURNBUCKLE

ASSEMBLING A PERIMETER FRAME

1 Cut the pieces

Cut frame pieces to length. You can butt the pieces together as you would fence rails and posts, but for a stronger joint, use rabbet joints (notches across the ends of boards) Cut the rabbets at both ends of the horizontal frame pieces, as shown above.

2 Assemble the frame

Assemble the pieces on a flat work surface. For added strength, use deck screws and weatherproof glue instead of nails. Whichever joinery method you choose, use a carpenter's square to make sure boards are perpendicular to each other as you join them.

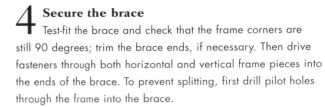

3 Make a brace

Set the gate frame on top of a 2 by 4 positioned diagonally from the bottom hinge-side corner to the top latch-side corner; mark the inside corners on the 2 by 4 as shown. To get the tight fit you'll need, saw the brace to length along the outside of the pencil marks.

4 Secure the brace

Test-fit the brace and check that the frame corners are still 90 degrees; trim the brace ends, if necessary. Then drive fasteners through both horizontal and vertical frame pieces into the ends of the brace. To prevent splitting, first drill pilot holes through the frame into the brace.

SECURING THE SIDING

1 Lay out boards

Test-fit siding boards, adjust as needed, and mark board positions on the frame. Then nail on the pieces or attach with screws, starting at the hinge side. It's simplest to let board tops run long, then cut them all at once.

ADDING THE SIDING. The instructions outlined here are for attaching vertical boards to a gate frame, but the procedure isn't much different for horizontal or diagonal siding.

If boards will be butted together, cut them to length and lay them vertically across the frame, working on the ground or another flat surface. Lay the first board flush with the edge on the hinge side; the last piece should be flush with the frame edge on the latch side. (Siding can overlap the latch side if it acts as a gate stop, as described on the facing page.) If not, you have three choices:

- Space the boards slightly.
- Use an additional board and cut a little from one edge of each board.
- Start at the middle with full-size boards and cut or plane the two end boards to fit flush with the frame edges.

For plywood or other sheet siding, lay the frame flat over the siding. Use a pencil to trace the frame's outside edges on the siding; then cut along the line.

Use nails or screws to attach your board or sheet siding to the frame.

2 Mark the top

Cut any curves or other shapes in the gate top after the siding is attached. To trace a smooth arc, make a guide with a nail and a piece of string, as shown above; draw other shapes freehand.

3 Cut board ends

Be sure there's no gate framing behind the cutting line; then make the top cuts with a jigsaw (shown above) or handsaw.

GATES FOR SLOPING GROUND

If the ground slopes markedly between your gate-posts, you should still make the gate frame rectangular, making sure each of the four corners forms a 90-degree angle. The bottom of the siding, not the bottom of the frame, should be sloped to follow the contour of the ground.

It's best if you hinge the gate on the downhill side. If the gate is hinged on the uphill side, it will tend to sag slightly and may drag along the ground.

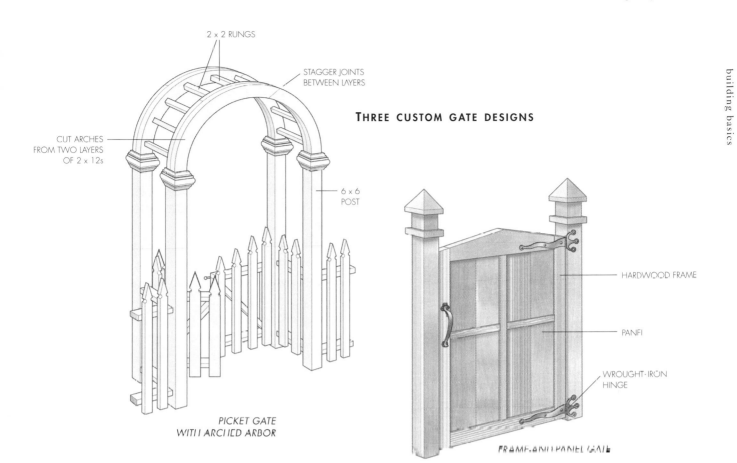

THREE CUSTOM GATE DESIGNS

2 x 2 RUNGS

STAGGER JOINTS
BETWEEN LAYERS

CUT ARCHES
FROM TWO LAYERS
OF 2 x 12s

6 x 6
POST

PICKET GATE
WITH ARCHED ARBOR

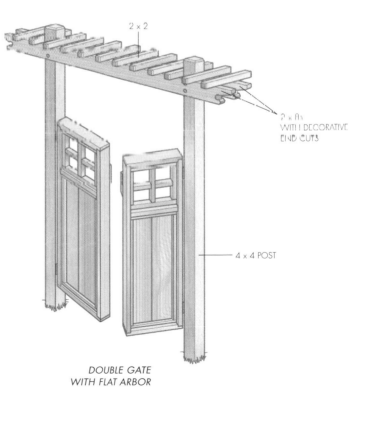

HARDWOOD FRAME

PANEL

WROUGHT-IRON
HINGE

FRAME-AND-PANEL GATE

2 x 2

2 x 8s
WITH DECORATIVE
END CUTS

4 x 4 POST

DOUBLE GATE
WITH FLAT ARBOR

Spacing gate pickets

Use a spacer board to ensure even spacing of
pickets, securing pieces one by one as shown.

HANGING A GATE

Installing your new gate is a three-part process: securing the hinges to gate and gatepost, installing the latch, and (in many cases) adding a gate stop on the latch side.

The following guidelines assume you're hanging your gate between two wooden gateposts. If you're attaching a gate to a masonry wall, you have two options: choose a lag-style masonry hinge embedded in mortar; or secure a wooden gate jamb to the masonry by means of expanding anchors (see page 112), then screw standard hinges to the jamb.

INSTALLING HINGES. When it comes to hinges, your first concern should be the size of the fasteners: screws should penetrate frame and gatepost as far as possible without coming out the other side. If the fasteners that come with your hinges are too short, replace them with longer, weather-resistant screws.

Once the hinges are secured to the gate itself, hold the gate in place in the opening to check the fit. (If the gate is too close to the posts to swing freely, plane the edge of the latch side as needed.) Attach the gate to the post and make sure it swings easily, opens all the way, and closes flush with the posts.

To help the gate close properly, you may wish to install a return spring (see page 123).

INSTALLING THE HINGES

1 Fasten hinges to gate
Position each hinge on the gate, mark the screw holes, and drill a pilot hole at each mark, using a bit that's slightly smaller than the fastener diameter. Screw the hinges to the gate frame.

2 Prop the gate in the opening
Have a helper hold the gate in place, or prop it in position with wood blocks or shims; mark the hinge screw holes on the post.

INSTALLING A LATCH. The next step is to install the latch assembly on the gate and the corresponding post. Latch designs—and installation methods—vary. A self-closing latch is shown at right; for other options, see page 124. Be sure that the latch design you choose aligns neatly with both gate frame and gatepost. Use screws or bolts that are as long as possible without coming out the other side.

ADDING A GATE STOP. Unless your chosen latch will do the job by itself, fasten a strip of wood vertically to either the latch post or the gate to stop the gate when it closes; this will keep it from swinging too far and loosening the hinges.

The stop can be attached to the back or the side of the latch post. The fence or gate siding can also serve as a stop by overlapping the gate frame or gatepost on the latch side. These possibilities are shown in the drawing below right.

INSTALLING A LATCH

To install a self-closing latch, first hold the latch in place on the gatepost and mark the screw holes. Drill pilot holes; then fasten the latch in place. Insert the strike into the latch and mark the screw holes on the gate. Again, drill pilot holes; then screw the strike to the gate frame, as shown.

3 Screw hinges to gatepost
First drill pilot holes for screws; then fasten the hinges to the post. Remove the shims and test the swing; make adjustments as needed.

GATE STOP OPTIONS

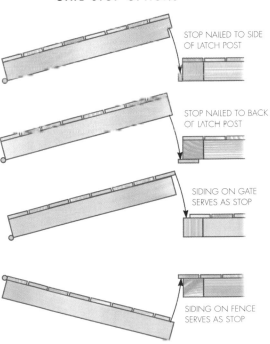

STOP NAILED TO SIDE OF LATCH POST

STOP NAILED TO BACK OF LATCH POST

SIDING ON GATE SERVES AS STOP

SIDING ON FENCE SERVES AS STOP

A SHOPPER'S GUIDE

Maybe they're not all that GLAMOROUS, but materials for fences, walls, and gates can produce beautiful end results—like those shown in "Great Fences, Walls & Gates," pages 11–59. Wood, masonry, and hardware products must be chosen carefully if they're to stand the test of time. The insider's knowledge you'll need to make good choices is the subject of the following pages. FENCING LUMBER COMES FIRST: decay-resistant species, like redwood and cedar, or pressure-treated lumber, are tops here. Masonry wall units include brick, block, and stone; poured concrete and mortar help other materials do their job. A great gate starts with quality hardwood, softwood, or prefab metal, plus sturdy, stylish hardware. WHERE DO YOU FIND these items? Home centers are carrying more and more products; for others, look to traditional outlets like lumberyards, masonry and garden suppliers, and specialty hardware stores. Ready to start shopping? Just turn the page.

Lumberyard Primer

Most fencing projects begin with lumber. And since wood is what takes the biggest bite out of your project budget, it pays to learn the fundamentals of lumber types and terms before you shop. This section will introduce you to the characteristics of different kinds of standard fencing lumber, explain how wood is sized and graded, and present options for other wood fencing products as well.

Basic components for wood fences are shown on page 63.

NOMINAL AND ACTUAL SIZES

Be aware that a finished "2 by 4" is not actually 2 inches thick by 4 inches wide. The nominal size of lumber is designated before the piece is dried and surfaced, so the finished size is a touch smaller. Here are some examples:

2 by 4 = $1\frac{1}{2}$" by $3\frac{1}{2}$"
2 by 6 = $1\frac{1}{2}$" by $5\frac{1}{2}$"
1 by 8 = $\frac{3}{4}$" by $7\frac{1}{4}$"
4 by 4 = $3\frac{1}{2}$" by $3\frac{1}{2}$"
6 by 6 = $5\frac{1}{2}$" by $5\frac{1}{2}$"

Sorting out your choices

For starters, lumber is divided into *softwood* and *hardwood*. These terms simply refer to the origin of the wood: softwoods come from conifers, hardwoods from deciduous trees. Because softwoods as a rule are much less expensive and more readily available than hardwoods, they are the usual choice for fencing.

Beyond these two basic categories, woods from different kinds of trees have their own particular properties. For example, redwood and cedar "heartwood" (the darker, denser part of the wood, from the tree's core) are naturally resistant to decay. This characteristic (combined with their beauty) makes these woods ideal candidates for fencing. Because they are costly and limited in supply, however, many landscape professionals use less expensive types of wood, such as Douglas fir or western larch, and apply a preservative or finish to make the wood more durable (see page 125). Using pressure-treated lumber is another way to reduce cost; for details, see the facing page.

SURFACED, ROUGH, RESAWN? *Surfaced lumber*, which has been planed smooth, is the standard for most construction. It's available in a range of grades (see following). Some lumberyards and home improvement centers also carry *rough lumber* (not surface-planed), typically in lower grades, with more defects and a higher moisture content. Rough boards are generally cheaper but more irregular than surfaced lumber.

Resawn lumber has texture added after the board has been dried, producing a pleasingly rustic appearance (and adding to the cost). Any grade of lumber can be resawn—a benefit where higher grades are needed for strength. And resawn lumber accepts stains particularly well.

Rough lumber is usually closer to the nominal size (see box at left), since it's wetter and hasn't been surface-planed. When measurements are critical, be sure to check the actual dimensions of any lumber before you buy it.

LUMBER GRADES. Lumber is sorted and graded at the mill. Generally, lumber grades reflect several factors: natural growth characteristics (such as knots); defects resulting from milling errors; and commercial drying and preserving treatments that affect strength, durability, and appearance.

Redwood is usually graded on the basis of both appearance and percentage of heartwood. Clear All Heart is the best and most expensive grade. B Heart, Construction Heart, and Merchantable Heart—in descending order of quality—are typical grades of pure heartwood.

Cedar grades, starting with the highest quality, are Architect Clear,

2 x 4
PRESSURE-TREATED LUMBER

2 x 4
ROUGH REDWOOD

4 x 4 CONSTRUCTION
HEART REDWOOD

2 x 4 PINE

Custom Clear, Architect Knotty, and Custom Knotty. These grades don't indicate if the wood is heartwood. To determine that, appearance is your guide: heartwood is darker and redder, while sapwood is paler in color.

The higher the grade, the more you usually have to pay. One of the best ways to save money on your fence project is to choose the most appropriate grade—not necessarily the costliest—for each component. Save the good stuff for where it shows.

PRESSURE-TREATED LUMBER. Though redwood and cedar heartwoods are naturally resistant to decay and termites, most other woods soon rot and weaken if they are in prolonged contact with soil or water. To solve this problem, less durable types of lumber (such as southern pine and western hem-fir) often have chemical preservatives applied under pressure to guard against rot, insects, and other sources of decay. These woods are less

expensive than redwood or cedar, and in some areas they're more readily available.

Pressure-treated (PT) wood is available in two "exposures." For lumber that will be next to the ground, like fence posts, the Ground Contact

2 x 4 HEM-FIR

6 x 6
PRESSURE-TREATED
LUMBER

type is required. Use the Above Ground type for other applications.

Working with treated lumber has its drawbacks. Unlike redwood and cedar, which are easy to cut and drive fasteners into, treated wood can be hard and brittle, and it can warp and twist. Moreover, some people object to its typical sickly green color (a reddish brown version is sometimes available) and the staplelike incisions that usually cover its surface (some newer types come without these marks).

Because the primary preservative used contains chromium, a toxic metal, you should wear safety glasses and a dust mask when cutting treated lumber and use gloves when handling it for prolonged periods. Opinion is mixed on whether pressure-treated lumber poses any health hazard, especially for children; this is probably less of a concern for fencing than it would be for decks or raised beds, since there is likely to be little direct contact with the wood.

Other wood products

Not all wood fences are created equal: some feature products other than those that come from the lumber stacks. Here's a sampling of readily available options.

PRECUT FENCE BOARDS. You'll find a selection of precut fence boards (see below) at most lumberyards and home centers. Those with squared ends are called "flat tops," those with angled tops "dog ears" (DE). Precuts usually come in 4-, 5-, and 6-foot lengths and in widths that correspond to 1 by 4, 1 by 6, and 1 by 8 lumber. Shop carefully; inferior sapwood and flaws may show up in precut boards. You can always find better grades in standard lumber—you'll just have to cut them yourself.

Precut pickets are available in a variety of simple patterns, depending on the manufacturer; you can buy them in prefab fence sections, too, with rails already attached. The pick-

ets are typically 42 inches tall and 2½ or 3½ inches wide, and often they come already primed with paint. Prefab panels are usually 8 feet long.

BENDERBOARD. For curved fences, try flexible redwood benderboard, typically about ⁵⁄₁₆-inch thick. You'll often find benderboard at landscape supply stores, where it's sold for use as garden edgings.

SPLIT WOOD. Rough split rails and grapestakes are used for rustic-looking fences. Unless you want to split rails from trees cleared off your own property, look in the Yellow Pages under "Fence Materials" for the nearest source of split rails. They are generally available at lumberyards, and some garden supply or farm supply centers stock them.

Redwood or cedar grapestakes are available in roughly 2 by 2 squares or as 1 by 3 slats, in lengths from 3 to 6 feet. The slats may have one rough side and one fairly smooth side for easier nailing. Because they're split from

"FLAT TOP" FENCE BOARD

"DOG EAR" FENCE BOARD

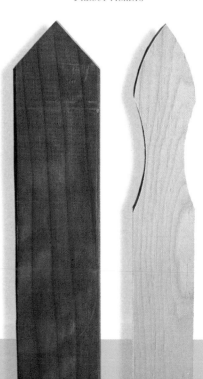

PRECUT PICKETS

logs, grapestakes have irregular, splintery edges (you may want to wear gloves when handling them). While grapestakes were originally split from heartwood, there is a trend today toward the use of sapwood, which has a tendency to decay rapidly when placed on the ground.

POLES. Fence poles come in various sizes, from 2 to 6 inches in diameter or even larger. The most widely available poles are smooth-turned on a lath, but in some locales you may also be able to buy poles in the rough, cut from saplings with bark and branches removed.

Six-inch-diameter poles are most commonly used as fence posts; they're available pressure-treated with a preservative for that purpose. Smaller-diameter poles, also called "palings" or "tree stakes," are used for stockade-type fencing.

6" PRESSURE-TREATED POLE

BAMBOO POLE

2" TREE STAKE

REDWOOD BENDERBOARD

CEDAR GRAPESTAKES

SPLIT-RAIL POSTS

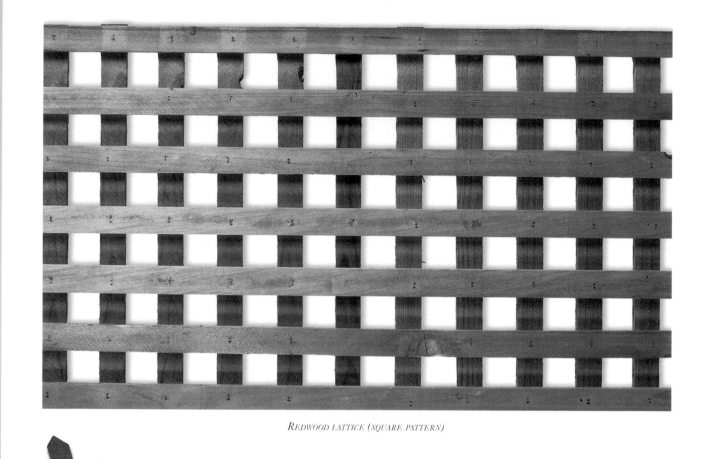

REDWOOD LATTICE (SQUARE PATTERN)

*REDWOOD LATTICE
(DIAGONAL PATTERN)*

1 X 2 LATH

LATH AND LATTICE. Wood lath means any thin, flat lumber that's available in long strips. Lath is typically about $\frac{3}{8}$ to $\frac{3}{4}$ inch thick and $1\frac{1}{2}$ inches wide. You can buy pieces individually or bundled.

Lattice consists of thin lath crisscrossed horizontally and vertically or on the diagonal. So-called "privacy panels" have the smallest openings. Lattice comes in both 4- by 8-foot and 2- by 8-foot panels. Most lattice has rough, open ends (see the facing page), but you can also buy preframed panels or separate lattice caps or posts to finish off these ends.

Lattice quality varies: sometimes you'll see loose grading terms like Architectural or Select. When shopping, examine the quality of both the lath itself and the fasteners that hold the lath together. You might prefer vinyl lattice (see page 110) to some inferior wood panels.

SHEET PRODUCTS. An old standby for solid panel fences and screens,

RESAWN SIDING PINE

HARDBOARD SIDING

exterior-grade plywood comes in standard 4- by 8-foot sheets, although panels up to 10 feet long are also available. Thicknesses range from $\frac{3}{8}$ inch to $1\frac{1}{8}$ inches; the most common sizes for fencing are $\frac{3}{8}$ inch, $\frac{1}{2}$ inch, $\frac{5}{8}$ inch, and $\frac{3}{4}$ inch.

Surface texture can be smooth, resawn, or grooved. You can buy plywood house siding unfinished, primed for painting, or prestained in a variety of colors. Don't buy interior grade plywood—the glues won't stand up to outdoor use.

Another option is *hardboard*, made of wood fibers rendered from chips of waste wood, bonded with adhesives under heat and pressure. Standard hardboard comes in 4- by 8-foot sheets, in thicknesses from $\frac{1}{8}$ to $\frac{1}{4}$ inch. Some hardboard house siding is prefinished and comes with a 25-year guarantee.

T 1-11 PLYWOOD

EXTERIOR-GRADE PLYWOOD

HARDBOARD SHEET

Metal & Vinyl Fencing

Wire is the most common fencing material other than wood, ranging in appearance from the purely utilitarian to a modicum of stylishness. Need something more ornate? Steel and aluminum are the modern prefab successors to ornamental wrought iron. Vinyl fencing is also available in a wide range of styles, including both metal and wood "look-alikes."

Wire fencing

Wire for exterior use is usually made of galvanized steel, sometimes coated with polyester or vinyl; it comes in a great number of mesh patterns and sizes as well as gauges (thicknesses), and often it's available in earth-tone colors. Extruded-plastic fencing—usually a mesh resembling wire fencing—can be used in many of the same applications as light wire.

Wire fencing is sold by the roll: widths (which translate to fence height) range from 2 to 5 feet; typical roll length is 50 feet. Some home and garden centers

WELDED WIRE MESH

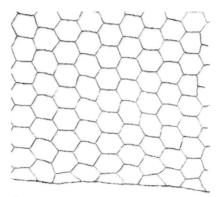

POULTRY NETTING

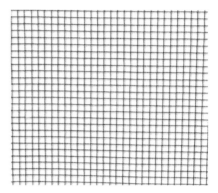

HARDWARE CLOTH

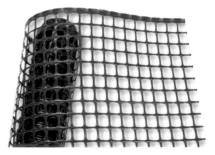

GREEN PLASTIC MESH

stock wire fencing in bulk and sell it by the foot.

Wire fencing can be attached to a wood framework (see page 79) or installed as part of an all-metal fence. For the latter, you'll want either light-duty metal stakes or—for heavier welded wire—heavy-duty T-posts; both are shown at left.

HEAVY-DUTY T-POST

LIGHT-DUTY STAKE

Chain-link fencing

Once considered a commercial and industrial fence material, chain link has infiltrated many residential landscapes. To relieve the stark, metallic look, vinyl-coated chain-link fencing is available in colors, most often black, green, and white. Chain-link wire comes in 50- to 150-foot rolls, typically in 4- to 6-foot widths.

Thin plastic or metal strips can be woven into the chain link to provide privacy and add a touch of visual interest to the fence. These slats, sold in rolls, are made in a variety of earth-tone colors.

Chain-link posts and rails are shown below at right. The framework consists of hollow, galvanized steel ter-minal (end) posts, smaller line (intermediate) posts, and still smaller top rails that span the distance between posts. Frame pieces range from $1\frac{3}{8}$ to $2\frac{3}{8}$ inches in diameter and come in a variety of gauges. You'll probably need to cut post and rail sections to length.

Chain-link fittings join posts to rails—it's much like assembling plumbing pipe. A selection of fittings is shown at right. These are sold individually, in bins, at most home centers and building supply yards. You can purchase a matching chain-link gate, too (see page 121).

PRIVACY SLAT ROLL

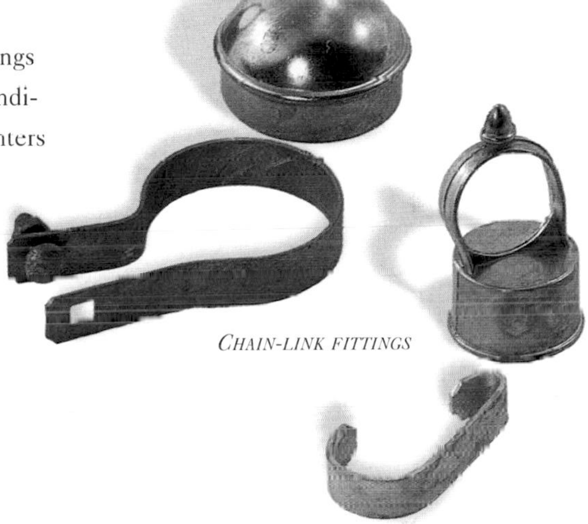

CHAIN-LINK FITTINGS

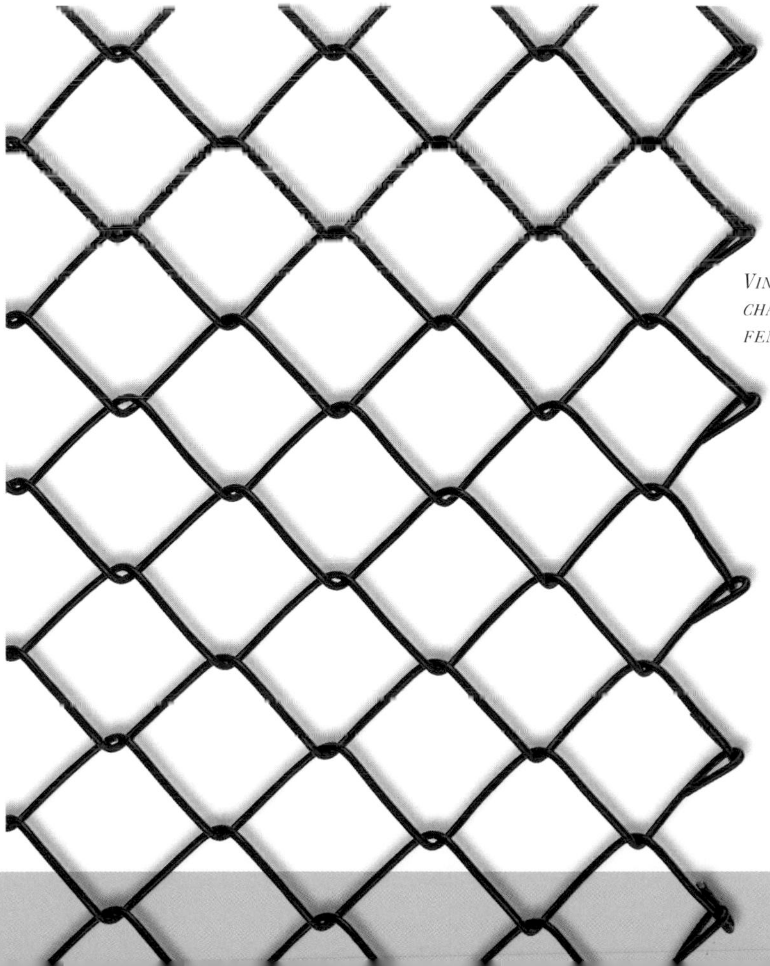

CHAIN-LINK RAIL AND POST

VINYL-COATED CHAIN-LINK FENCING

GREEN VINYL LATTICE

Vinyl fencing

Vinyl fencing comes in many of the same styles as traditional wood fencing: post-and-rail, post-and-board, picket, and various board fence replicas. Some vinyl fences can be installed by an experienced do-it-yourselfer; others are best assembled by professionals. Installation details vary depending on the manufacturer and the style of fence. Most vinyl fences come in kit form, with interlocking posts, rails, siding, and finishing details included—all parts cut to length and ready to assemble. A sample is shown at right.

VINYL FENCE

Once installed, vinyl fences are easy to maintain: they won't rust and peel, and since the color is integral to the vinyl, they don't need painting. (Vinyl doesn't take paint well, so be sure to choose a color you like.)

A few vinyl fences are stocked by some large home centers, but most are special-order items. Colors may be limited to white and brown.

Vinyl lattice, a weatherproof version of wood lattice, *is* common at garden centers. Like its wood counterpart, vinyl lattice comes in 4- by 8-foot panels; unlike wood, it's available in a number of colors—typically white, brown, gray, and green.

WHITE VINYL LATTICE

Ornamental metal fencing

Ornamental fencing once meant ornamental iron—those elegant wrought-
iron masterpieces that graced the
mansions of the Victorian era. Today
the term encompasses not only traditional wrought iron but ornamental
steel and aluminum as well. Designs
in all three metals range from ornate
handcrafted works of art to sleek
modern grillwork that comes in prefabricated sections.

There are contractors who specialize in the installation of custom metal
fences, since the job is somewhat complex. Or you can install prefabricated
sections yourself.

Home centers often stock preassembled rail and grill assemblies;
the typical unit size is 8 feet long by
either 4 or 5 feet high. The ladderlike
sections attach to matching posts with
special brackets and fasteners. Colors
are limited: usually black and/or white.

PREFABRICATED STEEL GRILL

*WROUGHT-IRON
SPIKES*

STEEL POST

Fence Fasteners

Nails, screws, and framing connectors are the "glue" that holds a fence together. The fasteners you choose help create the strength of your finished fence, and they can also affect its appearance.

Nails

Hot-dipped galvanized, aluminum, or stainless steel nails are best for outdoor construction, because they're rust-resistant. Galvanized is the norm; aluminum and stainless are pricey. As for the type of nail, you can use common or box nails for most jobs. Heavy-duty common nails have a thick shank—a feature that makes them more difficult to drive but increases their holding power. Choose a finish nail when the head shouldn't show; drive it nearly flush, then sink the rounded head with a nailset.

A nail's length is indicated by a "penny" designation ("penny" is abbreviated as "d," from the Latin *denarius*). These are the equivalents in inches for the most frequently used nails:

3d = 1¼"	4d = 1½"
6d = 2"	8d = 2½"
10d = 3"	16d = 3½"

COMMON NAIL   *FINISH NAIL*

Choose nails about twice as long as the thickness of the material you'll be nailing through. Most fence framing is secured with 8d and 16d nails, most 1-by fencing boards with 4d or 6d nails.

Screws

Though they're more expensive than nails, coated or galvanized screws offer some advantages. They don't pop out as readily as nails; and since they aren't pounded in, you don't have to worry about hammer dents.

Galvanized deck screws are surprisingly easy to drive into redwood and cedar if you use an electric drill or screw gun. They come in several colors, including gray, gold, brown, and red. Drywall screws (also called multipurpose screws), usually black, come in smaller sizes than deck screws but are usually less weather resistant. These two screws are not rated for shear (or hanging) strength; for that, use a

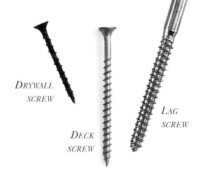

DRYWALL SCREW   *DECK SCREW*   *LAG SCREW*

heavy-duty lag screw. The lag screw has a square or hexagonal head and is driven with a wrench or a ratchet.

Bolts

For heavy-duty fastening, choose bolts. Zinc-plated steel is the classic choice for outdoor use, though aluminum and brass bolts are also sold. Bolts go into predrilled holes and are secured by nuts.

The machine bolt has a square or hexagonal head, a nut, and two washers; it must be tightened with a

CARRIAGE BOLT

MACHINE BOLT   *EXPANDING ANCHOR*

wrench at each end. The carriage bolt, less industrial in appearance, has a rounded self-anchoring head that digs into the wood as the nut is tightened. Expanding anchors allow you to secure wooden members—like a fence post—to a masonry wall.

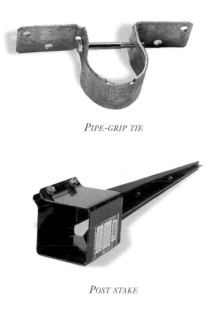

PIPE-GRIP TIE

POST STAKE

Framing connectors

The photos on this page show a collection of fence-friendly framing connectors. Galvanized metal connectors include fence-rail brackets, angle brackets, post caps, mending plates, and various reinforcing straps. Pipe-grip ties allow you to secure wood rails to a metal post; metal post stakes support light-duty fence posts without the need for concrete below.

POST-TOP POSSIBILITIES

Some pieces of wood and a few saw cuts can spruce up an otherwise prosaic fence post or rail. For some starter ideas, see page 75. Browse through the color photos in "Great Fences, Walls & Gates," pages 11–59, for inspiration. For other ideas, take a close look at the fences you pass in your daily travels.

Prefab post caps, available in growing numbers, may be wood, metal, cast ceramic, or plastic—or a combination of materials. Some models have pegs or screws that

slip into holes drilled in post tops. Others have shallow flanges that slip over the posts like the lid of a shoebox—glue these in place with weatherproof adhesive.

You can also add interest to your fence by adding a fence cap—either made at home or purchased where fencing materials are sold. For ideas, see page 77. Something as simple as adding a piece of 2 by 6 across the top of the fence can be a big improvement.

ANGLE BRACKET

REINFORCING STRAPS

MENDING PLATE

FENCE-RAIL BRACKET

Blocks & Bricks

For fast, affordable masonry wall construction, it's hard to beat concrete blocks. These rugged units make strong decorative and structural walls, and working with them is comfortably within the capacity of the do-it-yourselfer. Stackable retaining blocks are even more user-friendly. Traditional brick and adobe still have their place, too.

The basic block

The tried-and-true concrete block is much less expensive than brick or stone. It's also considered less attractive than those materials. This isn't a problem if you use the block wall as a core over which a coating of brick or stone is applied as a veneer (see page 91). Or you can add plastering stucco (page 91) to the concrete-block core.

The large size of concrete blocks—8 by 8 by 16 inches is standard—makes for rapid progress in building. In addi-tion to the standard size, blocks come in 4-, 6-, and 12-inch widths.

Standard blocks are molded with regular heavy aggregate and weigh about 45 pounds each. Lightweight cinder blocks, available in some areas, are made with special aggregates. Either type is suitable for residential projects.

Whatever the size and weight of the basic block, a whole series of frac-tional units, end blocks, and cap blocks is likely to go with it. With a little planning, you may never have to cut a block.

DECORATIVE SCREEN BLOCK

CONCRETE BLOCKS

Decorative blocks

Most manufacturers also make a variety of decorative blocks designed to produce surface patterns that catch the play of light, enhancing a wall's appearance. These sculptured blocks can be combined in various ways to produce overall patterns in a wall.

Slump blocks are made with the use of a press that gives them an irregular appearance similar to that of trimmed stone or adobe. Some have patterns cast in relief on their face shells. Dimensions are somewhat variable, in contrast to most other blocks.

Split-face units are broken apart in manufacture and resemble cut stone. Combining several sizes enhances the effect.

Screen or grille blocks are designed to be laid on end. They form patterned screen walls that admit light and air while still affording some privacy.

Glass blocks represent the opposite end of the masonry spectrum from earthy brick or stone. Typically, you can find them in 6- to 12-inch squares and in clear, wavy, or crosshatch textures. Installation can be tricky, but several new products are aimed at do-it-yourselfers.

Stackable retaining blocks

Mortarless, stackable concrete blocks —often called "retaining blocks" at home centers—are the new wall units in town. Their distinguishing feature is that they're often held in place simply by a system of interlocking lips, grooves, or pins; two types are shown at bottom right. These blocks, which are backfilled or mortared as you go, are ideal for do-it-yourselfers. They look great, too.

Shop around and you'll find both straight and curved units, plus a variety of profiles, colors, and textures—and even "planter" blocks (they have open pockets for plants and soil). Some interlocking systems require mortar or caps on top; others don't.

GLASS BLOCKS

ADOBE WALL BLOCKS

STACKABLE RETAINING BLOCKS

Adobe

Rugged adobe walls add color, texture, and—due to their thickness—summer coolness to an enclosed patio. The most common wall-block size is 4 by 8 by 16 inches, about the same size as four or five clay bricks put together. Of course, adobe is considerably more cumbersome than brick: the blocks weigh up to 45 pounds apiece. Installing them is a workout.

Historically, earth-and-straw adobe blocks were doomed to decay, victims of the combined forces of summer heat and winter rain. Today, however, adobe is made with either an asphalt stabilizer or Portland cement to keep the blocks from dissolving. Although found almost exclusively in

Arizona, New Mexico, and Southern California, adobe can be used effectively in almost all parts of the country. Outside the West, though, delivery charges can make it quite costly.

Bricks

Made of various clay mixtures, bricks were once molded by hand but now are usually extruded. The clay is forced through a die, then cut to size with wires. After drying, the bricks are fired in a kiln to harden them.

Basically, bricks fall into two categories: common brick and the more expensive face brick. *Common brick* is less consistent in size, color, and texture than face brick. *Face brick* is made of specially selected materials and fired at a higher temperature, which makes it stronger. Common brick is often used for both paving and rustic garden walls. Face brick is excellent for formal walls.

Used brick has uneven surfaces and streaks of mortar that can look espe-

cially attractive in an informal setting. Manufactured used or "rustic" bricks cost about the same as the genuine article and are easier to find; they're also more consistent in quality than most older bricks. *"Split paver" bricks* are roughly half the thickness of standard bricks—they're great for veneer walls. *Concrete "bricks,"* available in classic red as well as imitation "used," are increasingly popular as substitutes for the real thing; they're also less expensive.

The standard modular brick is about 8 inches long by 4 inches wide by 2⅜ inches thick. Other sizes may

CONCRETE "BRICKS"

be available at larger brick-yards. It's common for brick dimensions to vary, so when size is critical, take your tape measure along and measure the bricks before buying.

For areas with severe climate variations, especially where the bricks will be exposed to heavy rain and frost, choose SW (severe weathering) grade.

CONCRETE AND MORTAR

Though they're not as glamorous as brick or flagstone, cement products often are just as important to both fence builders and masons. Concrete holds fence posts, makes wall footings, and forms low walls (though this is an advanced job). Mortar joins stone, brick, and block.

CONCRETE INGREDIENTS

Concrete facts

Concrete is a mixture of Portland cement, sand, aggregate, and water. Cement is the "glue" that binds everything together and gives the finished product its hardness. The sand and aggregate (usually gravel) act as fillers and control shrinkage.

Buying bagged, dry ready-mix concrete gets expensive, but it's also

MORTAR SACK

READY-MIX CONCRETE

convenient, especially for small jobs like setting a few fence posts. The typical posthole requires about $\frac{2}{3}$ cubic foot of concrete, and it just happens that a 90-pound sack of ready-mix makes $\frac{2}{3}$ cubic foot.

For larger jobs, ordering materials in bulk and mixing them yourself is the economical way to go. Pouring a wall footing? Some dealers supply trailers for wet ready-mix that you can haul behind your car. On a grander scale, a commercial transit mix truck can deliver enough concrete to allow you to finish a large concrete wall or an adjacent patio in a single pour.

Follow this formula for regular concrete (the proportions are by volume):

> 1 part Portland cement
> $2\frac{1}{2}$ parts sand
> $2\frac{1}{2}$ parts aggregate
> $\frac{1}{2}$ part water

Use clean construction sand, not beach sand; the aggregate can range from quite small to about $\frac{3}{4}$-inch in size. Water should be of drinkable quality, neither excessively alkaline nor acidic, with no organic matter.

Mortar recipes

Mortar recipes vary according to the intended use, but the ingredients are always the same: cement, hydrated lime, sand, and water.

The most common kind of mortar for general use is Type N. The following proportions (by volume) approximate Type N and make a good all-around mix for most jobs:

> 1 part Portland cement
> 1 part hydrated lime
> 6 parts sand

Add just enough water to produce a plastic—but not runny—mortar.

If you prefer, you can buy more expensive ready-mix mortar by the sack at masonry yards and home centers. Though recipes vary by brand, most manufacturers produce a mortar similar to Type N. If your job is small, ready-mix may be your best bet.

Stone

Stone walls have the appeal of a thoroughly natural material, and most are very durable. Marble and granite are igneous (volcanic) rock, and they create the hardest surfaces. Sandstone, limestone, and other sedimentary stones are more porous; they usually have a chalky or gritty texture. Dense, smooth slate is a fine-grained metamorphic rock. The availability of

RIVER ROCKS

stone types, shapes, sizes, and colors varies by locale.

Stone's primary drawback is that it can cost up to five times as much as brick or concrete. It takes a lot of time and effort to quarry, trim, haul, and store stone—and more to truck it to your yard. Local materials, especially rubble rock, are almost always the most economical option.

Stone styles

There are four basic types of wall stone: rubble, semidressed, flagstone, and ashlar.

The uncut stones used in *rubble masonry* are typically rounded from glacial or water action; examples (often igneous in origin) include granite and basalt river rock and fieldstone. Large, fairly uniform stones can be stacked and held together with mortar; small stones and pebbles can be mixed into mortar and used as a veneer over concrete blocks. Rubble stone is more casual and decidedly less expensive than most trimmed stone. If you

SONOMA FIELDSTONE

have a local source, you may even be able to get it for free.

So-called *semidressed stone*, such as cobblestone, has been roughly shaped. Veneer stone is semidressed stone that's specially cut for veneering concrete block walls. It's a uniform 4 or 6 inches thick with a flat back that allows for easy installation. Technically, *flagstone* is any semi-flat stone that's either naturally thin

GRAY FIELDSTONE

or split from rock that cleaves easily. Flagstone works well in almost any garden setting. Stacked flagstone (either dry or mortared) looks the most natural, but you may need a lot of it—which can be expensive. The other option is to apply flagstone as veneer.

Fully trimmed *ashlar stone* can be nearly as easy to lay as brick. Ashlar stone is usually sedimentary in origin, with sandstone probably the most commonly available. Sandstone's quality of stratification makes it easy to split and trim. When harder igneous stone, such as granite, is cut and trimmed for ashlar masonry, the cost is likely to be quite high.

Buying stone

If you calculate the volume of your wall, your dealer can help figure the quantity of stone you'll need. Some dealers sell it by the cubic yard, simplifying your order; others sell it by the ton. Cut stone and flagstone may be sold by the square foot. To find the volume of your wall, multiply its height by its width and length. To convert cubic feet to cubic yards, divide by 27.

Home centers usually stock only a small range of stone. For other sources, check the Yellow Pages under these headings: "Building Materials," "Landscape Equipment and Supplies," "Quarries," "Rock," and "Stone-Natural."

COBBLESTONE

SPLIT WALL STONE

VENEER STONE

ASHLAR STONE

FLAGSTONE

Gate Materials

Some gates blend in, while some beg for attention. Either match your gate to a fence or wall, or add drama with a gate built from different materials. Integrate your gate's siding with the gate posts, or fashion a surround from a contrasting wood or masonry material.

You can build your own gate, buy a ready-made version, or have a craftsperson make a one-of-a-kind

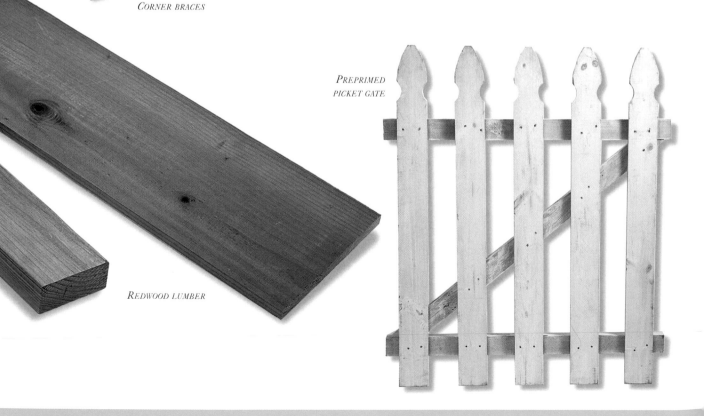

CORNER BRACES

statement for you. For a gallery of gate ideas, browse through pages 36–43. For design specifics, turn to pages 92–99.

Wood for gates

In selecting lumber for wooden gates, choose from standard fencing lumber (see pages 102–104) or, if you wish, add finer hardwoods.

Basic gate components are shown on page 93. Lumber for a gate frame should be straight and free of defects. Even slightly warped lumber can throw the whole gate out of alignment. Choose wood that has been pressure-treated with a preservative, or use the

heartwood from a decay-resistant species such as redwood or cedar.

Most gates have diagonal braces made from 2 by 4s covered with facing material. Lighter frames—made from 2 by 2s or 2 by 3s with no diagonal bracing—can be used if the siding is exterior plywood, hardboard, or some other sheet material. Diagonal bracing is not usually required in these cases because the sheet material itself will keep the frame square.

You'll want to buy the straightest and driest lumber you can for a gate; if only green or damp lumber is available, be sure to let it dry out thoroughly before using it.

PREPRIMED PICKET GATE

REDWOOD LUMBER

Gates to go

Most home centers stock gates to complement their other prefab fence offerings. In wood, both board- and picket-fence gates are common. Utilitarian chain-link gates serve chain-link and wire fences; most steel and vinyl fence lines also include matching gate designs.

Also be on the lookout for recycled or antique gates. Remember that gates aren't necessarily different from doors, windows, or outdoor screens—all of which might be candidates for your perfect gate. Salvage yards, flea markets, and antique fairs are all potential sources of gates.

Handcrafted gates

Of course, a skilled craftsperson can fashion a gate from whatever design you can dream up—providing it's structurally sound and reasonably lightweight and you can find the appropriate hardware for hanging it (see pages 122–123).

Carpenters, woodworkers, woodcarvers, or landscape contractors may specialize in outdoor gates. For metal gate fabricators, look in the Yellow Pages under the heading "Gates" or "Iron, Ornamental Work."

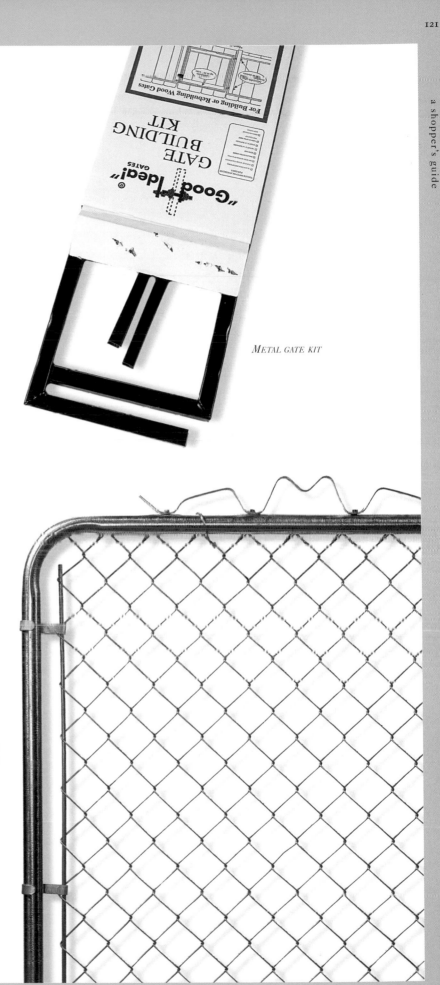

METAL GATE KIT

CHAIN-LINK GATE AND HARDWARE

Gate Hardware

Hinges hold up your gate and allow it to swing smoothly; the latch stops the gate and keeps it shut. Good hardware is critical to both the look and the function of your finished gate. Here's what you need to look for.

Hinges

Inadequate hinges are the number one cause of gate failure. It's better to use an overly strong hinge than one that's not strong enough. Gate hinges should be rust- and corrosion-resistant, which means galvanized steel, wrought iron, or another baked-on, weatherproof finish.

Several standard hinge styles are shown here. All of these do a good job, provided they are sized for the weight of the gate and attached with screws that are long enough. Many packaged hinges come with fasteners that are too short for a heavy gate. Use screws that go as far into the wood as possible without coming out the other side. It's best to put three hinges

BRASS BUTT HINGE

on gates over 5 feet tall or more than 3 feet wide. A turnbuckle (shown on the facing page) can help shore up a wide, heavy gate that has questionable hinge support.

The nature of both your gate siding and the gate post will influence your choice of hinge—or vice versa. (For details on gate design, see pages 92–99.)

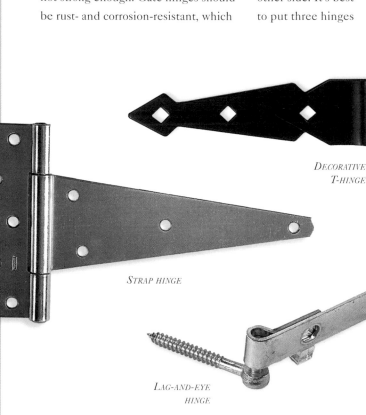

DECORATIVE T-HINGE

STRAP HINGE

LAG-AND-EYE HINGE

SELF-CLOSING HINGE

IT'S AUTOMATIC

On driveway gates, electric gate openers often are installed for security and convenience. Similar in principle to the garage door opener, these devices can be operated by a switch in the house (usually in conjunction with a two-way intercom), a keyed switch or keypad outside the gate, radio controls inside a car, or a combination of these. Models are available for single and double swinging gates and sliding gates.

Electric locking devices and intercoms can also be installed on walk-through gates so that house occupants can be selective about visitors.

Such units are just beginning to show up at home centers. Otherwise, try the Yellow Pages under "Door Operating Devices." The dealer you choose can recommend the best unit for your gate.

This entry-gate design includes a discreet security panel, housing both intercom and keypad.

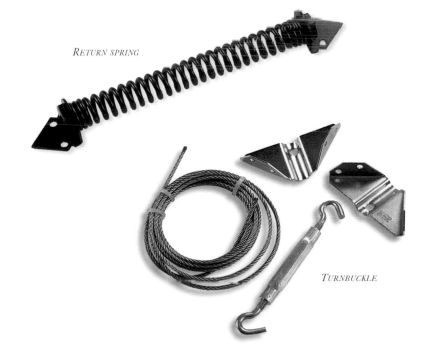

RETURN SPRING

TURNBUCKLE

You may also want to buy hinges that match the latch, and sometimes this calls for a revision in the gate design. A knowledgeable hardware dealer can assist you with the fine points.

If a fence is used to confine small children, self-closing hinges (shown at left) are a worthwhile investment. Springs in the hinge mechanism automatically close the gate, which otherwise might be left ajar.

If you find that your gate doesn't stay shut, install a return spring. This heavy-duty spring will automatically pull the gate closed after you pass through.

HOOK-AND-EYE LATCH

Latches

Because the latch is the device people reach for to open and close a gate, it is often the focal point in the gate design. So it's a good idea to carefully consider both the appearance and the mechanical operation of any latch you're considering.

The photos at right show the most common latch styles. Note that not all latches are suitable for every gate and gate post. You must either choose a latch that works with your gate design or, if you've found a latch you love, adapt the gate design to work with the latch. For more on gate design options, see pages 92–99.

You can special-order more ornate styles or have a custom-made latch fabricated by a metal worker. If you're building a wooden gate, you might also devise a wooden latch. For a substantial frame-and-panel gate, look at exterior door knobs and locks, too.

Though latches usually serve to keep a gate closed, some can hold it open. Two examples shown are the simple hook-and-eye latch and the fancier cane bolt.

Whether you buy a latch or make your own, be sure it's sturdy enough for the gate and the rough handling it will have to take. Use the longest screws or bolts possible when attaching the latch assembly. Like other fence and gate hardware, latches should be rust- and corrosion-resistant. That usually means galvanized steel, wrought iron, or another weatherproof coating.

CANE BOLT

HASP LATCH

TOP LATCH

SLIDING BOLT LATCH

BARREL BOLT

SELF-CLOSING LATCH

THUMB LATCH COMPONENTS

FENCE FINISHES

There's no substitute for decay-resistant wood such as heart redwood or pressure-treated lumber where posts or rails come in contact with soil or are embedded in concrete. However, applying a water repellent, a semitransparent stain, a solid-color stain, or paint can protect other parts of a fence and preserve the wood's beauty.

Whatever product you choose, it's best to try it on a sample board before committing your entire fence. Always read labels: some products should not be applied over new wood, while others may require the application of a sealer first.

Water repellents. Also known as water sealers, these products help keep wood from warping and cracking. They may be clear or slightly tinted; the clear sorts do not color the wood, instead letting it fade over time to gray. You can buy either oil- or water-base products, many of which include UV-blockers and mildewcides. Traditional oil-base finishes generally last longer, but water-base versions are less toxic and easier to clean up.

Don't use clear surface finishes such as spar varnish or polyurethane on outdoor lumber. Besides being expensive, they wear quickly and are very difficult to renew.

Semitransparent stains. Available in both water- and oil-base versions, semitransparent stains contain enough pigment to tint the wood's surface while still letting the natural grain show through. Usually one coat is sufficient. You'll find traditional grays and wood tones as well as products to "revive" an unpainted structure's natural wood color or dress up pressure-treated wood.

Solid-color stains. To cover a structure in a solid color, you can choose either stain or paint. Stains for fences or siding are essentially thin paints; they cover the wood grain completely. For custom tints, you can usually mix any paint color you choose into this base.

Paint. Covering wood in an opaque coat of muted to vibrant color, paints hide defects so thoroughly that they let you use lower grades of lumber.

Most painters recommend a two-step procedure for outdoor structures: you first apply an oil-base (alkyd) prime coat, then follow it with one or two topcoats of water-base (latex) enamel. Ideally, the primer should cover all surfaces of the fencing lumber, so it's best to prime before assembly. Apply topcoats after the structure is complete.

Shown at right, from top to bottom: unfinished redwood board, clear water sealer, tinted oil-base repellent, semitransparent gray stain, and red solid-color stain.

design & photography credits

design

GETTING STARTED

4 Design: Kelly Frink and Tag Merrick; Builder: John Mikiska/ Star Masonry **6** Design: Leishman & Barnes **7** Landscape designer: Delaney & Cochran **9** Architect: McKee Patterson/Austin Patterson Disston Architects

GREAT FENCES, WALLS & GATES

13 Design: Bud Stuckey **14 top** Architect: Alejandro Ortiz, Alejandro Ortiz Architects **14 bottom** Architect: William B. Remick **15 top** Design: Lisa

Moulton **15 bottom left** Designer/builder: Mark O'Neil/ Woody's Fences **15 bottom right** Design: Charles Prowell; Builder: Tim Moore **16 top** Design: Garden Architecture/ Robert Trachtenberg **16 bottom** Landscape architect: Louis Marano **17 bottom left** Design: Ruth Chivers **17 bottom right** Designer/builder: David Milligan **19 bottom right** Design: Father Sergious Gerken; Builder: Benjamin Smith **22 top left** Design: Sue Kenah **22 bottom** Design: Billie Gray **23 bottom** Design: John Ermacoff/Prolific Garden Landscaping **24 top right and bottom left** Design: Christine Swanson **25** Designer/builder: Thomas Swartz

27 Landscape designer: Topher Delaney **28 top right** Landscape architect: Naud Burnett **31 top** Design: Webb Landscape **31 bottom left** Builder: Tom Murphy **31 bottom right** Landscape architect: Louis Marano **32 top** Landscape designer: Topher Delaney **33 top** Architect: Michael Harris Architecture; Lighting designer: Becca Foster Lighting Design; Contractor: Pete Moffat Construction **33 bottom** Landscape designer: Cristin Fusano Landscape Design **34 bottom** Tile artisan: Debra Yates; Landscape architect: Raymond Jungles **35 top** Design: J. R. and Julie Means **37** Design: Van Chaplin **38** Design: Bud Stuckey **39 bottom** Design: Trachtenberg Architects/David Trachtenberg; Construction: Garden Architecture **40 top** Design: Garden Architecture/Robert Trachtenberg; Blacksmith: Jefferson Mack **40 bottom** Design: John Nethercott & Co. **41 top right** Landscape architect: Peter Curé/Arterra; Gate fabrication: Paco Saucedo/ Art-Mex Iron Works **41 bottom** Gate artist: David Burns/Copper Gardens; Fence contractor: Owen Flynn/Flynn's Construction **42 top left** Garden designer: Ryan Gainey **42 center right** Design: William Derringer **42 bottom** Design: Walpole Fence **43 top left** Design: Charlie Thigpen **44** Design: Robert Cowden **45 right** Designer/builder: David Milligan **46 bottom** Design: John Harlow Jr./Harlow Gardens **47** Jeremy Smearman **48 top** Design: Jay and Rosemary Hill **48 bottom** Design: John Greenlee **49 top**

Landscape designer: Debra Huffman **50 top** Design: Shelley Cash **52** Post caps: Peterson Ceramics **53** Design: Laura White and Jude Hellewell **54 top** Landscape designer: Topher Delaney **54 center left** Fence light: Artistic Cedar Post Company **54 bottom right** Design: Joleen and Tony Morales **55** Landscape designer: Kathleen Shaeffer/Great Gardens **56 top** Landscape architect: Alana Markle **57 top left** Design: Debra Burnette, Steve Martino, J. Barry Moffitt **57 top center** Design: Bill Martin **57 bottom** Design: Pratt Brown **58 bottom right** Tile artisan: Marlo Bartels Studio of Laguna Beach

A SHOPPER'S GUIDE

123 top right Architect: Steven Sanborn; Landscape architect: Tom Klope

BACK MATTER

126 bottom Landscape designer: Cristin Fusano Landscape Design **127 top** Design: Warren Deckard and Paul Dubois

photography

Jean Allsopp: 28 top right, 39 top left; **Scott Atkinson:** 125; **Christian Blok:** 57 top left; **James Boone:** 50 top; **Marien Brenner:** 29; **Susan Burdick:** 52 bottom; **Van Chaplin:** 37, 42 top left, 43 top left, 47, 57 bottom; **Glenn Christiansen:** 27; **Crandall & Crandall:** 7 top, 36 bottom; **Robin B. Cushman:** 1, 2, 17 top, 18 top left, 22 top left, 43 top right, 51 bottom, 57 top middle, 59 top; **M.A.P./Arnaud Descat:** 50 bottom; **Alan & Linda Detrick:** 19 top left, 28 top left, 60; **Derek Fell:** 24 bottom right; **Frank Gaglione:** 85 bottom right, 86–89 all, 90 top, middle, and bottom right, 91 all, 114 top right, 115 middle; **The Garden Picture Library:** 17 bottom left,

43 bottom left; **Tria Giovan:** 22 top right; **Steven Gunther:** 8; **Jamie Hadley:** 9, 17 bottom right, 20 bottom, 31 bottom left, 33 bottom, 35 top, 40 bottom, 41 bottom, 45, 105 bottom left, 107 bottom and top left, 119 right third from top, 127; **Lynne Harrison:** 56 bottom; **Philip Harvey:** 7 bottom, 10, 32 bottom, 33 top, 58 bottom right, 65 top right, 83 bottom left, 114 bottom, 115 top right, 117 top, 118 left, 119 top left; **Cheryl Himmelstein:** 14 top; **Saxon Holt:** 18 bottom right, 21 top, 42 top right, 46 top, 49 bottom right; **James Frederick Housel:** 54 left; **Dency Kane:** 19 middle left; **Randy Leffingwell:** 48 bottom; **David Duncan Livingston:** 54 top; **Allan Mandell:** 20 top left and right; **Charles Mann:** 35 bottom, 56 top, 59 bottom left; **David

McDonald/PhotoGarden, Inc.:** 53, 54 bottom right; **E. Andrew McKinney:** 15 bottom right, 16 all, 19 bottom right, 23 all, 24 bottom left and top right, 25, 31 bottom right, 32 top, 39 bottom, 40 top, 42 middle right, 62, 65 bottom four, 66 all, 68–77 all, 79 all, 83 top, middle, and bottom right, 90 bottom left, 92–99, 100, 103–104 all, 105 top, right three, and bottom middle, 106 all, 107 top right, 108–111 all, 113 all, 115 bottom, 117 bottom, 118 right and bottom crossover, 119 right top two, 120–124 all, 126; **N. and P. Mioulane:** 49 bottom left; **Terrence Moore:** 4 bottom, 28 bottom, 41 top right, 46 bottom, 49 top; **M.A.P./C. Nichols:** 43 right, 51 top right, 58 bottom left; **Jerry Pavia:** 12, 18 bottom left; **Norman A. Plate:** 15 top, 31 top, 44 bottom,

48 top, 59 middle right, 78, 112 all; **Lanny Porvo:** 34 bottom; **Tom Rider:** 15 bottom; **Susan A. Roth:** 22 bottom, 24 top left, 42 bottom, 44 top, 57 top right; **Thomas J. Story:** 13, 38, 55; **M.A.P./F. Strauss:** 58 top left; **Tim Street-Porter:** 34 top; **Brian Vanden Brink:** 30, 41 top left; **Paddy Wales:** 6, 21 bottom, 58 top right, 67; **Jessie Walker:** 18 top right; **Deidra Walpole:** 26 bottom left; **Darrow M. Watt:** 116; **Jeff Weissman:** 14 bottom; **Peter O. Whiteley:** 51 top left; **Tom Wyatt:** 80, 85 left and top right

index

Numbers in **boldfaced type** refer to illustrations.